Practitioners Manual

Herbert L Beierle

Practitioners Manual

**Compiled—Edited—Written
By Herbert L Beierle**

First Edition 1987
Revised Edition 1995

COPYRIGHT © 1995 BY
UNI PRESS
Campo California 91906

PRINTED IN THE UNITED STATES OF AMERICA

TABLE OF CONTENTS

Page

List of Books 8

Dedication 9

Preface 10

To the Reader 11

Introduction 13

About the Writers 19

    Each theme has the series of essays in the following order of dedicated metaphysical doctors who are ordained and accredited licensed practitioners: Ellen Jermini, Stefan Strässle, Ingeborg Puchert, Katarina Suter, Sylvia Maria Enz, Ilse Wenk and Robert Rettel.

    Each essay has a paragraph introducing its author and bridging these seven theme essays into one useful work for easy application.

*S*even practicing practitioners have written essays on each of the following fifteen themes:

Theme	Title	Page
1	Primary Function of a Practitioner	23
2	Everyone Is a Practitioner	39
3	A Practitioner's Responsibility	55
4	A Practitioner's Prayer	71
5	The Practitioner the Creator	87
6	The Practitioner's Principle	103
7	One Day in a Practitioner's World	121
8	The Value of Positiveness	139
9	The Practitioner a Friend to All	157
10	The Practitioner a Medical/Spiritual Healer	173
11	The Practitioner a Minister	191
12	The Secret of Miracles	207
13	The Practitioner's Charisma	225
14	The Practitioner's Food	243
15	The Practitioner's Goal	261
	Conclusion	279

Also by Herbert L Beierle

The Art and Science of Wholeness
Song of the Spirit
Illumination, Handbook of Ascended Masters
Autobiography of God
The Relative
The Relative/Absolute
ABSOLUTE
Practitioners Manual (edited by)
Ministers Manual (edited by)
A Gift from Self to Self
I Am Number One
My Inner Journey
The Weathering
Quiet, Healing Zone
Why I Can Say I Am God
How to Give a Healing Treatment
Practice Reality
Three Hour Meditation
The Law of Cause and Effect
The Inexhaustible Laughter of Heaven—BLISS
Gist (edited by)
Uni Press Publications
Syllabus

Many of these books are available in
German, Italian, French and Russian.

ISBN 0-940480-26-3

All rights reserved. No part of this book may be reproduced or transmitted in any form or by any means, electronic or mechanical, including photocopying, recording or by any information storage and retrieval system, without permission in writing from the Publisher.

UNI PRESS
1101 Far Valley Road, Campo California 91906 USA

DEDICATION

To Earth's Friends

*M*an cares about man. Everyman is a practitioner, everyone. Historically our hearts reach out to our fellow beings in time of stress and our first desire is to bring peace to their lives by our caring love. It matters not who the other may be—such is the heart of each of us. All of us belong to the race of humans and as such know one another and befriend our fellows as we would be befriended. Hence we call all *friend*. This book is dedicated to Earth's population of humans—our *friends*, wishing all peace!

—*The Compiler*

PREFACE

*T*his book is a practical guide for ministers, practitioners and laymen alike. Published by the Uni Press, it is an uplifting manual affirming we are the creator and master of our world and our thought.

The book is unique in that it is written by seven practitioners who share experiences out of their own everyday life to guide and inspire the reader-practitioner in researching their solutions.

We realize that in every circumstance we create in life, we handle it according to our attitude based upon our character and on our education. As we read the illustrations given, we see how each practitioner handles *problems* in a powerful and successful way.

The reader will find the *Practitioners Manual* a supportive friend sharing precious gifts for every circumstance. Each chapter stands on its own. Reading this book makes living life a successful adventure.

—*Ellen Jermini, PhD*
President of the University of Healing

TO THE READER

*T*o achieve the whole we synthetically listen to the examples of a host of our fellows deducing from their lives the most meaningful illustrations which reveal each theme of this volume.

The art of philosophy is our search for wisdom and the art of psychology is awareness of our response to life's wisdom. Combining these two grand arts the writers here allow the reader to recall from their own experiences examples for the application of each concept or theme.

The purpose for sharing the genius of these men and women most of whom are monks working and living in the Absolute Monastery in Campo, California, is to offer entrance to the high road of sincere practice in the field of being a sharing/caring/loving/nonjudgmental practitioner. To many this seems an improbable and impossible task. Yet, as the reader lives through the examples of each dedicated, disciplined, determined, diligent, onepointed, nonjudgmental practitioner, whose writings appear here, an overwhelming warmth will arise in the reader, and most important of all, the realization is born that each indeed is a viable practitioner and always has been so competent.

As with all manuals, the *Practitioners Manual* is designed as the *starter kit* for the reader to go on and experiment, share, love and absolutely unconditionally give to his *friends*—all the world.

Happy practicing wondrous practitioners!

—Herbert L Beierle, PhD

INTRODUCTION

A practitioner is a professionally trained and skilled person who knows what and who he is and practices that awareness. The probity of the practitioner is a demonstrated circumstance in all areas of his life.

As a master technician of the rules of the game of spiritual awareness a professional practitioner no longer hopes his ministrations function as does the amateur, he knows the principle upon which he bases all of his understanding always brings definite results.

The foundation of the practitioner's activity is the Law of cause and effect. *This Law is defined as:* **whatever cause is put into motion** (*mentally, physically or spiritually)* **an effect equal to the cause issues forth inevitably, inexorably, and inexplicably.**

Nonprofessionals use the Law also, but do not use it knowingly.

Too often people *give up* in their plight while utilizing positive mental attitudes. This *giving up* is in fact putting another cause into motion contrary to an earlier cause and the later cause being current and abided in more enthusiastically (continuously), results. Professional practitioners know this and have learned to be onepointed in their use of the Law. They have learned to be

13

humble to the inexplicable working of the Law, for the Law functions often beyond reason and logic to achieve its purpose. The tide of its action, once initiated is so unfailing, so inevitable, its conclusion cannot be avoided or prevented. To plead with its inexorable action proves unyielding as it accomplishes its function.

The *Practitioners Manual* discloses the genius of seven worldwide practicing practitioners writing on various aspects of the practitioners' craft.

In a book, a classroom, a spiritual training center or in a monastery the ability to teach the art of practitionership is at best an incomplete effort. The work of training one to be a practitioner must fall upon the individual shoulders of the individual student practitioner.

To effectively work as a practitioner the one who would train in this art and science learns these disciplines:

Humility

Onepointedness

Discipline

Determination

Dedication

Diligence

Humility The practitioner completely gives up all control to the principle, trusting in the integrity of the Law as each counselee/friend relies upon the probity of the counselor/practitioner. This trust and humility of the practitioner remains steadfast regardless how long it takes for the treatment to be revealed.

Onepointedness The practitioner remains single objective minded. He has no other expectation than the working out of whatever cause he has placed in motion: indefatigably. To be able to consistently retain the initial enthusiasm of onepointedness is a trained awareness in the professional practitioner. For all about him the conditions speak contrary to his treatment of choice and the professional must keep his vision alone on *his* cause and his cause alone. To do this takes selfabnegation of the purest kind since human nature would falter and fail.

Discipline By discipline here is meant selfdiscipline. The ability to hear what you want to hear. To see what you want to see. To think what you want to think. To do what you want to do. To live as you want to live. To speak as you want to speak. On the surface all this sounds pretty wonderful—wonderfully free! However, it is just the contrary. It is controlled. Controlled by ourself.

A disciplined professional practitioner only hears his inner divine voice speaking, nothing else has any sound.

A disciplined professional practitioner sees his inner self reflected back wherever he looks and that which he sees is his perfect ideal outpictured!

A disciplined professional practitioner has communication as the *one mind* and in this omniscience knows all and thinks out of the archetypal creation of all thought and lives in the state of pure illumination at all times.

A professional disciplined practitioner has actions arising out of his divine nature complimentary to his inner wisdom.

A disciplined professional practitioner expresses life, for in him is all the power of the universe and utilizing this omnipotence the professional experiences life beyond human comprehension.

A disciplined professional practitioner does not question the wisdom that comes to his thoughts but vocalizes inherent genius through a dynamic charismatic powerful voice.

Determination The professional practitioner knows who and what he is—to what extent: totally; in what position: his allness; in what quality: his highest; in what nature: his probity (intrinsic character and qualities: integrity). The professional practitioner knows he is the absolute in its who and what! defined to the maximum.

Dedication The professional practitioner leaves the teeming herds of humanity to find his inner self. The professional practitioner sets himself apart for the special purpose of living his awareness of his divine nature. He is committed absolutely to being his creative divine self responsible only to his indwelling wisdom.

Diligence The assiduous behavior of the professional practitioner is marked by his persevering attitude to living by the fundamentals of the Law of cause and effect, constantly attentive to its fulfillment.

An illustration often used in the spiritual training center of the Absolute Monastery is:

A person is operating the printing press and it is functioning perfectly after many very careful adjustments. The abbot comes along. He asks: *Turn off the press, pick up the paper clip on the floor, give it to me; then start the press again and continue printing.* If the *printer* can instantly turn off the press and pick up the paper clip and give it to the abbot, and start the press again WITHOUT feelings of irritation, anger, disgust and possession for the task at hand, he is well on the path of being a professional practitioner. For his work did not possess him. He was able to freely shift gears from a complex work to what could appear to be a totally unimportant task, and THEN return to the task without irritation in his soul, truly a master consciousness indwells that person.

A training center in these spiritual arts allows for these experiences. Alone it is unlikely one

17

could enjoy this demonstration. Also, in any *business* for profit it would be unprofitable to do what we do at the Absolute Monastery in training practitioners.

As soon as a monk, practitioner trainee, learns a task, he is transferred to another work experience. This does not engender efficient work loads being completed, but the primary task of the Monastery is the development of the spiritual genius of each monk. Secondly is the operation of the organizations: the Absolute Monastery, the University of Healing, the Church of God Unlimited, the University of Philosophy, the Far Valley Ranch Meditation Center, the Far Valley Ranch, the Worldwide Healing Ministry, the Church of God Unlimited International (with churches around the world), the God Unlimited Practitioners (with accredited professional practitioners in every corner of the globe), the Global Seminars, and the Uni Press (publishers of books and publications worldwide, the monthly *GIST* magazine, Italian ABSOLUTE Newsletter and the German ABSOLUTE Newsletter).

We are nonpossessive of our dynamic multinational nonprofit corporations functioning in Europe and America and around the globe.

We practice our art and science as professional practitioners. ∞

ABOUT THE WRITERS

*T*he writers of the *Practitioners Manual* are licensed practitioners and come from diverse backgrounds to share their expertise and wisdom with the reader. Here are pictures and biosketches on each professional.

Dr Herbert L Beierle from Wisconsin and California is dean and founder, and chairman of the board of the multinational universities as nonprofit-educational-religious-charitable corporations: University of Healing, University of Philosophy, Church of God Unlimited and the Absolute Monastery. Ordained in 1948 he edited and published newspapers and magazines for over 40 years, served in Silent Unity and ministered in Unity, Congregational, Methodist, Religious Science and God Unlimited Churches throughout the United States and conducts seminars throughout the world. Dr Beierle is author of over a dozen books, numerous pamphlets and other publications, and a teaching professor of philosophy in California.

Dr Ellen Jermini of Germany, Switzerland and America is the chief executive officer of the multinational corporations: the Church of God Unlimited, the University of Healing, the University of Philosophy and the Absolute Monastery. Being the abbot of the Absolute Monastery and an ordained minister she supervises the spiritual life of the monks, the affiliated churches and all UNI students. An enthusiastic speaker and writer she has lectured bilingually around the world and authored many articles and portions of books. To her joyous life belong her two children and five grandchildren.

Dr Stefan Strässle from Switzerland and the United States serves as the director of European operations of the University of Healing, University of Philosophy, Church of God Unlimited and of the Absolute Monastery. An ordained minister, Dr Strässle is a minister-at-large serving in Europe. He conducts seminars and lectures in Europe and America. Author, businessman, and world traveler, Dr Strässle teaches and writes on spiritual healing.

Dr Ingeborg Puchert from Germany, Italy and the United States serves as secretary of the University of Healing and University of Philosophy, Church of God Unlimited and the Absolute Monastery. She is secretary of these multinational corporations. Prior to her ordination she was a director in a Japanese shipping corporation with offices in Germany. She translates seminars into Italian and German and takes secretarial responsibility for the corporate business of the Church, the Monastery and the UNIS*. Her writings abound in the metaphysical field.

Dr Katarina Suter from Switzerland, Australia and the United States serves as director of New Zealand operations and graphic arts director for the multinational corporations: University of Healing, University of Philosophy, the Absolute Monastery, and the Church of God Unlimited. A world traveler, Dr Suter is a minister-at-large in Asia and New Zealand. She has translated numerous books and articles from German to English and English to German. She is a successful healing practitioner and an acclaimed author on spiritual healing.

Dr Sylvia Maria Enz from Switzerland and the United States is an active spiritual practitioner in the Absolute Monastery where she serves as vice president of the multinational corporations including the University of Healing and the University of Philosophy, where her excel-

---

* UNIs—University/universities. This is a common European term to denote a university or universities.

lence as an English/German translator has brought her worldwide laurels. Professor Enz is a proctor, and an international lecturer and author of positive philosophy.

Dr Ilse Wenk from Germany and the United States, former NATO employee, English, German and French seminar translator of the University of Healing, University of Philosophy, Church of God Unlimited and the Absolute Monastery in Germany, Switzerland, Austria and Italy. She is treasurer of these multinational corporations. She translates the UNI textbooks into German for use of students of the multinational educational organization and UNIs. Her stage acting and radio careers admirably suit her as she presents seminars worldwide and writes on spiritual healing.

Dr Robert Rettel of Luxembourg, Europe, a long time computer genius, is European minister-at-large of the Church of God Unlimited, University of Healing, University of Philosophy and the Absolute Monastery. Dr Rettel is a professional globetrotting practitioner of spiritual healing. He is a wellknown representative of the multinational universities and educational-religious organizations. His writings are widely acclaimed.

∞

Theme One

PRIMARY FUNCTION OF A PRACTITIONER

*P*ractitioners for the purposes of this program are people who have dedicated their lives to being at one *with and as* the perfect archetypal purpose of living on Earth and specifically seeing all beings on Earth expressing this perfect calling: the practitioner sees himself complete; then the practitioner sees all creation whole.

Principle Versus Law

*T*he practitioner's principle is defined as the Law of cause and effect!

Primary Function of a Practitioner

This is too simple a definition, albeit quite true.

Just as the *law* of mathematics is not mathematics, and the *law* of physics is not physics, so the LAW of cause and effect is NOT the principle.

The two, principle and Law, are so intertwined, intermeshed, and used by the principle (the Law does not use the principle, the principle uses the Law) that here we find the dividing line.

The Law is just the Law. It is not the principle and the Law does not make anything happen. The Law is a system through which the principle is performed and expressed, but without the principle *putting the Law to work* the Law would remain dormant and ineffective.

From this point of view we see that the principle includes far more than just a mechanism for accomplishing its purposes. The principle is the allness, the principle is the expression and still the nonexpression of all, the principle exists and expresses and does so regardless the presence of the Law or its lack of being present. The Law has but one purpose and that is to establish causes. The Law is not the cause nor the effect it establishes. The Law is the expression of the principle's decision to carry out its purposes.

While the principle is not the thinker behind all thought, in truth there is no thinker behind anything, there is only isness. For if there were a thinker thinking positively and relatively, there could not be an infinite principle which stands regardless of anything. The absolute expression would be watered down and the relative or human standards would be the reality domain.

The reality domain is where all just is, indefinable, inseparable, ONE! As such no identity is present and no nonidentity is present. This is inconceivable for the relative thinker. Yet it is true. No values exist for nothing has value. All just is and cannot be otherwise.

Ah the dilemma of seeking to put labels on anything.

For now let's enjoy what our practitioners have shared with us and step by step walk into the awareness of something far greater than we have yet conceived in our finite thinking.

Dr Ellen Jermini describes the primary function of a practitioner as one who fully believes in himself.

Selfconfidence

As we talk of the primary function of a practitioner, we first understand who and what is a practitioner. A practitioner is one who practices living what he believes about himself and his world. He lives a fulfilled beautiful life and is master of his creation. He knows who and what he is—God, the allness, the absolute—and reflects this inner knowingness in his world as a perfect living example.

The primary function of a practitioner is to lift his consciousness about those who come to him

Primary Function of a Practitioner

for guidance, prayer, treatment, religious functions and services, and for spiritual healing. In his high state of consciousness, in his excellence of being, he creates his world by his own charisma, by the love and light he shines forth through his inner knowingness, and through the wisdom of beingness. He guides his view of everyone in his world to a new understanding, a new level of awareness and thereby unfolds the native divinity within. This is the main and only function of a practitioner or any metaphysical minister: to know himself and those who come to him as a reflection of his pure thinking.

In one of many experiences in this relationship I remember a fourteen year old boy, the son of a friend of mine, who was taken to hospital for an inexplicably high fever, an indefinable illness. Days go by and his condition remains unchanged. I hear about him and immediately take charge of the situation. I look beyond the illusion of illness and see the young boy, an excellent tennis player, whole and perfect. I see him out on the tennis court enjoying exciting games, being a winner in life. Two days later I hear from his mother that the fever had miraculously disappeared and that the young fellow had taken over his normal life.

We create our world in the image of our own belief, in the joy and innocence of pure being, in the love and selfappreciation of a divine wonderful being, we practice the truth about ourselves. This as practitioners we keep steadily in our mind in every moment and in every circumstance of life.

As we deal with child or adult, any friend, we always remember who and what we are and see in our creation the perfection and goodness of our own self. We know that all is one and that what we see we are, the master and creator of our perfect world.

Dr Stefan Strässle describes the primary function of a practitioner as one who emphasizes understanding and use of the Law of cause and effect.

Law of Cause and Effect

A practitioner's primary function is to recognize and reveal who and what he is first within himself and then to create it in all his creation.

With great delight I remember an example of a perfect practitioner's work on behalf of one of my friends. A few months ago I received a phone call telling me of the diagnosis my friend's doctor had made: cancer. I immediately went into prayer-meditation and first realized the perfect, divine idea out of which I created my own physical body. Visualizing my own perfection I was able to create my friend's body in the same image: healthy.

It was a couple of days later when my friend called and informed me about her wondrous recovery. The doctors thought of it as an absolute miracle and were without words. To me as a practitioner it was the simple use of the one universal Law: THE LAW OF CAUSE AND EFFECT.

Primary Function of a Practitioner

We create everything in the universe through this very Law. We think a thought or cause and experience the equal result. The Law works under all circumstances. It is judgmentalless and unconditional which means that it brings forth whatever it is we put into motion—beneficial or unbeneficial—by our thoughts, words and actions. The Law is definite and always works according to our innermost thoughts.

A practitioner's treatment always works because we return to the source, the indwelling presence of the divine within ourself and through the Law call forth wholeness, perfection, prosperity or any of the wonderful conditions a practitioner's friend may desire to experience.

As practitioners we always *heal* ourselves first. We always recognize first who we are and then draw forth that realization/knowingness in the life of our friend asking for treatment, for all of life is a mirror of our own consciousness and we can only see in another what we are.

Dr Ingeborg Puchert describes the primary function of a practitioner as the practice of spiritual mind treatment.

Spiritual Mind Treatment

*T*he primary function of a practitioner is the practice of spiritual mind treatment **about him-**

self. The practitioner is well acquainted with the eternal principle, the Law of cause and effect. This is the basis for spiritual mind treatment. The practitioner lives up to the eternal principles. The practitioner is a living example of moral integrity, loving givingness and perfect wholeness. The life of the practitioner reflects a flawless state of awareness.

We practitioners affirm in thinking and saying the purity of our consciousness: *To the pure, all is pure* and know that out of our pure consciousness we see purity in everything and every circumstance.

Purity is a state of awareness we practitioners achieve through constant control of our consciousness. This state of awareness we keep up through constant meditation and introspection. The purity of our awareness we see reflected in the way our life and affairs express.

In our function of practitioners we encompass the highest achievement of spiritual understanding. We practitioners fulfill our primary function of bringing about the results of the requests for treatment we accept. We do the treatment from within and with all of our heart and soul: we see it done!

I bring the following example: I accept a request for treatment for a lady friend in Europe. She wants to walk without pain in her right leg. While I treat for myself I recognize within me total wholeness and perfection and see it reflected in my friend. I see myself as the friend in the state of original purity and wholeness. I enfold her in my blessings. I love myself and shower my powerful

Primary Function of a Practitioner

love on her. I receive the confirmation of the outcome of my treatment: My friend enjoys her original state of perfect health.

Our primary function as practitioners is the enjoyment of being the spiritual center of love, joy and harmony in our world. A community is blessed through the presence of us as practitioners. We practitioners act as loving balancers and catalysts wherever we are. From within we generate the energy for the inner light and let it shine outwardly.

Dr Katarina Suter describes the primary function of a practitioner as the awareness of self and being a catalyzer for everyone.

Divine Catalyzer

*T*he primary function of a practitioner is to reveal the divinity within himself and to catalyze it in the ones who come to him for guidance and sharing.

We know that each being on planet Earth has one purpose and that is to be aware of his true nature which is God, the divine, the absolute and be it. We call our nature many names and mean the same by it: the oneness of all creation. In this awareness we are all practitioners.

We express outwardly what we know as true inwardly. We are the living example of the truth about ourselves.

The expression of our true nature is the primary function, the essence of a practitioner's life. We have opportunities to express our task as a living example every instant of our life.

One day during my meditation walk I passed by the swimming pool and looked at the wonderfully crystal clear blue water. My attention was caught by a little lizard lying on the bottom of the pool without any movement. I quickly fetched the net with the long handle and lifted the lizard gently out of the water. I set it on the decking and looked at it. It looked as though dead. I talked to it and said: You are whole and perfect. I see you running around in the desert, enjoying a wonderful lizard life. As I had finished my meditation walk I again passed by the pool and my little friend the lizard had left. This experience was an innovation to me that as I am aware of my wholeness I create everyone in my world as a reflection of myself.

As a practitioner we are aware that we create each experience in our life as an exercise. We confirm our divinity through seeing all creation in the light of truth. The truth is that we are whole and perfect in body, mind and spirit; that we express our Godself in every situation of life and that we are aware of who we are and live it. In looking at ourselves through the eyes of truth we realize that we look through the same eyes at our creation and see our pure reflection. A practitioner's primary function is being and expressing who he is!

Dr Sylvia Maria Enz's essay describes the primary function of a practitioner as practicing the principle.

Practicing the Principle

The fundamental *function* of a practitioner is to **practice**. Many of us have taken piano and typing lessons. When we listened to an hour of explanations and demonstrations for the right finger strokes we are sent home to practice. Now it is up to each one to practice what he has learned.

We have a swimming pool. Often I watch our younger people diving so easily in the water. I decided to learn it too and to do it step by step. I let a friend show me how to hold my body, especially my head and hands. I tell myself that I feel absolutely comfortable with jumping in the water headfirst. I practice this everyday and soon I feel so good and comfortable in diving that I have a hard time to remember my former reluctancy.

To draw a parallel to the practitioner in the spiritual truth is easy. We have in us allknowledge intrinsically and we come to planet Earth to practice what we know. We know the truth about ourselves and practice it as visible effects in our world. We are the creators of our world and it is our responsibility as to how we create it. We create our world by the use of the Law of cause and effect.

Every thought we think has an effect. Every thought that we have ever thought is a cause and unfailingly shows a result unless we choose to put a different cause in motion. We as a practitioner are aware of every thought we think, of every cause we put into motion. We do this first and primarily in our own consciousness—because that is where our world happens (is born).

We create this world, this dimension of time and space to demonstrate mastership in it. We create every situation in our world for exactly this reason—as a learning tool to be master in it. The world we create and experience happens in our own consciousness alone. What we see we are. What we think we are. Where our thinking is, there is our experience. We determine what we practice: being the master of every thought we think. We create our world and our friends in it by the reflection of our thought.

We outpicture what we believe about ourselves and our world outpictures what we believe about ourselves. We as practitioners live in a most magnificent world. We live in our world of reality, where every thought is a thought of truth, a thought of: love, kindness and peace. We as practitioners see the truth reflected in everybody that enters our world. Our world is pure and perfect, beautiful and full of love; love that we are, that everybody is.

So our primary function as practitioners is to look at our world and recognize the truth, the goodness and the love in everybody in our world. A practitioner practices his world *into* supreme beingness.

Dr Ilse Wenk's essay describes the primary function of a practitioner as pure meditation.

Pure Meditation

The primary function of a practitioner is to practice spiritual purity and spiritual mind treatment. A practitioner practices spiritual purity within his Godself. His role is a most important one. A practitioner is absolutely concerned with his own awareness. He meditates and sees that the world is pure and perfect. A practitioner lives in his high state of sincerity and purity. A practitioner recognizes that the world is whole and perfect because he lives wholeness and perfection.

As a practitioner living in Europe I worked with many friends.

One was separated from her husband and was very downcast. I first treated myself and then talked to my friend about the Law of cause and effect. I told her that we think every moment of our life myriad thoughts and that it is beneficial when we are aware of them. I told her that every thought is very important. The Law of cause and effect—every thought is cause—is being applied by everyone every moment of our life. With every thought I put the Law into motion. So I use the Law. My friend and I had many meetings and I talked over with her the experiences she had while beginning to live the Law of cause and effect consciously.

This was some time ago and she now lives vitally valiantly alone, absolutely new. She is thankful for the consciously chosen beautiful life she now lives.

The primary function of being a practitioner is to introduce myself and my friend as myself to the Law of cause and effect and talk with myself and myself as my friend about every thought I think. The thought is the most important and the only cause of my life. What I think I am.

A primary function of a practitioner is to practice love. We the practitioner prepare ourself by learning to love ourself absolutely and then all our friends in our world. Friends WE call those who are named patients in medicine.

As practitioners we are responsible for every thought we think and for every word we speak and for every action we make. We are well prepared as practitioners because we practice in a daily schedule of dedication, determination, diligence, discipline, humility and onepointedness which is very important for the work of any practitioner.

The primary function of a practitioner is to first reveal the divinity in ourself then see our friend revealing the divinity in themself—our reflection.

Dr Robert Rettel describes the primary function of a practitioner as selfbalance.

Mental Balance

*A*s a practitioner we practice spiritual purity and spiritual mind treatment. We see ourselves and our world from the highest point of view: we see purity, integrity, wholeness and perfection. We visualize our world and absolutely everybody as completely whole and perfect right now. In our universe we see integrity and purity. In every situation, in every condition—we see only purity.

With all our heart, with our full attention, with total dedication, we look with purity; thus we create purity, as with all our thoughts we dwell on purity. We think pure thoughts all the time, we speak pure words, we act with a pure heart.

We see purity all the time and in absolutely every situation.

We recognize purity in all areas of life. We see everyone physically, mentally and spiritually whole and perfect. We see perfect bodies, we see mentally balanced people. We see ourselves and all the people in the total universe as a perfect expression of our inner divinity. We recognize our true nature, our Godself.

We practice spiritual purity. Spiritual, for we *work* with just one instrument, one tool: our thought. We activate our God nature to its fullest; and so we speak our word: We are God. We are totally and always concerned with our own state of awareness; we recognize with every thought and every word the world we live in as pure and perfect. In this integrity and sincerity we place the right causes in motion relative to ourselves and to our people for the highest good of all. We thus fulfill the primary function of a practitioner.

In the face of an apparent negative situation at work, I start a treatment program for myself: I visualize myself and every person involved as pure and perfect beings. I see a beneficial outcome for me, for all the people in this situation. And the situation is pure; the working conditions are excellent and I am total, pure joy at my work.

◆

In everything humanity does it first attempts to say it is not responsible for its world. This is the greatest sin to which man is heir!

The primary function of a practitioner is to know he is fully responsible for his world and everything which happens in it. The practitioner's world includes EVERYTHING of which he is aware. The practitioner's world has all the experiences of his five senses, regardless whether he may feel—oh God why me—or if he thinks: I did nothing to bring this into my life! EVERYTHING is ours by our cause! Nothing: **notwithstanding!**

Once we accept this truism we can humbly move beneficially to set worthwhile causes, worthwhile dreams/desires, and worthwhile creations in the universe as we know it. This is responsibility at its highest and best.

Primary Function of a Practitioner

Now we can say with the master teacher, Jesus the Christ: **Oh God, for this was I prepared!**

∞

Theme Two

EVERYONE IS A PRACTITIONER

*E*very being is a practitioner because every being thinks and acts. This very thinking establishes causes which set into motion all conditions and actions in our lives. Regardless how we try to avoid responsibility for our thoughts, we alone set forth the pattern of every moment of our individual life.

If our values are joy and love, we think only these thoughts and experience only these effects. However, if we say we think only love and joy and hypocritically judge the appearances of the world as loveless and joyless—such is our *new* cause and its subsequent effect.

This is why it is so important to recognize everyone is a practitioner. That way we take responsibility for our individual expression and existence.

Dr Ellen Jermini lists an influence which we sometime allow to take control of our world and how to be master of it.

Being aware

*E*veryone is a practitioner. We practice living what we believe about ourselves and our world. What is it we really believe and think about ourselves? We believe, for example, that we are successful beings and so we practice being successful. We practice by being disciplined, dedicated, determined and diligent in our every moment thoughts, in our words and deeds, we practice being aware of using the great universal Law, the Law of cause and effect. We indeed recognize the causes we put into motion for our own fortune.

Everyone is a practitioner because everyone uses the Law beneficially—or unbeneficially—for his own success, or his own defeat in life. We know that we alone are the creators and masters of our world dependent on the cause we put into motion for our own advantage or disadvantage. We choose being poor, rich, healthy, ill, happy, unhappy, we alone make the choice. We choose whatever we like and feel comfortable with yet always being a practitioner, always using the universal Law, for that what we want to experience. We know that onepointedness is the basis for any achievement in life and to be successful in life we naturally put our concentration on success, on a specific goal we have in mind.

I recall my first class of elementary school. Together with 30 girls I learn to write and read. We all learn with the same teacher, we all follow the same system the teacher uses as a learning tool for us: diligence, discipline, determination and total dedication. Some girls learn quickly, some slowly. Some immediately read fluently and some take time. Everyone being free for his own limited—unlimited success. All is a matter of choice based on our belief; as we face it nonjudgmentally all is good; all just is.

For this reason everyone is a practitioner. It is up to us to define what results as a practitioner we want to have. We practitioners know that we are God, that God is all, that God is omniscient, omnipresent and omnipotent and that whatever we do, we do in the wisdom of our God presence.

We are beautiful people, we are successful people, as we practice to be successful, as we put our attention on being that what we are. It is done unto our belief!

Life can only mirror back to anyone what he reflects out to the world (his mirror) his belief about himself. Dr Stefan Strässle relates that as we know what we believe we effectively live that belief.

What I Believe

All of life is a learning experience. Everyone may look at everything from the point of view of spiritual growth and expansion of consciousness. Every being has come to planet Earth to remember who and what he is and to live and express it fully.

Living and expressing who and what we are is an individual yet universal experience. It is individual in so far as we live in a physical, relative world—where conditions, circumstances and things are continually changing which means that we as practitioners of who and what we are outwardly express ourselves in many different ways. However, we are all universal beings. From that point of view we inwardly express ourselves as one cosmic consciousness.

Everyone practices what he believes. Our life is a perfect reflection of what we believe about ourselves. This is the role of a practitioner: he expresses what he believes. This is true for everyone. We all have beliefs, attitudes and thoughts which *belong* to our personality and character. These beliefs are very powerful in our consciousness and reflect themselves moment to moment in our life and experience.

We create our world and draw into our experience exactly that which is in our consciousness. Everyone is really a practitioner!

One winter I spent a vacation in the Swiss Alps. I went skiing to the top of some of the highest mountains in eastern Switzerland, close to the Austrian border. We stayed in cabins and met other skiing groups. There was talk about the weather, snow conditions and possibilities of avalanches. When I heard this I surrounded my group with the white light of love. I did the same when we were on tour or wherever else we were. The next day we enjoyed a beautiful tour to the top of a 12,000 foot mountain. The view was gorgeous and skiing downhill in the powder snow was even more beautiful. We had a super time. It was only later that we heard that one group of ski tourists—staying at the same cabin as we did—almost created themselves buried in an avalanche on the very route we took. They saw and heard the avalanche coming and were able to turn aside so that the snow passed them by.

This illustration demonstrates so perfectly how we all are the creators of our world. We create ourselves on the same mountain, at the same time yet we create two totally different circumstances!

Everyone is using the one universal Law while practicing his beliefs: THE LAW OF CAUSE AND EFFECT. We all use the Law to accomplish our dreams and desires as well as we use it to demonstrate our beliefs, attitudes and thoughts whatever they may be.

We all are practitioners whether consciously aware of it or not. We all have beliefs, attitudes and thoughts within ourselves and by that very fact become practitioners using the Law to outpicture them in our world.

The perfect practitioner is the one who is consciously aware of being a practitioner and positively makes the choice

to practice perfection, harmony, peace, wisdom, love and prosperity in his everyday life.

Elusive as it can be, truth is the only reality. A practitioner knows and lives the truth of his own being and sees it expressed in his world, says Dr Ingeborg Puchert.

Truth Is Always Truth

*E*veryone is a practitioner. Wisely we create everyone as a practitioner. This is the truth about ourselves and what is the truth about ourselves we claim and affirm as truth about everyone. This is a confirmation about ourselves for we know who and what we are. We are practitioners and in everyone we see a practitioner, the *pure reflection of what we are.* We call everyone practitioner for we are it from within. This is the true nature of our being and of everyman.

We are omniscient, omnipresent and omnipotent. We are practitioners and treat being aware of who and what we are. We live from the highest level of our awareness and bring into existence every circumstance which we think. We work through the Law of cause and effect. Our life and affairs are the mirror of our awareness. We are aware of our spiritual beingness for all is spirit. We love ourselves and fill our mind with thoughts of love. We experience the power of unconditional love.

We polish the facets of our inner diamond and let it sparkle through our eyes. We do a marvelous work on ourselves and let shine our inner light. We are the light in our world and uplift ourselves as we see uplifted the friends for whom we treat. We practitioners of the Church of God Unlimited treat for ourselves and are a living example of the healing power within. The same healing power we see in everyman. We truly are that which we proclaim about ourselves, we are practitioners under every circumstance. Whatever we do for others, we do for ourselves and we do it with delight.

Being a practitioner means to us having a disciplined way of thinking. We create **by thought** everything in our world. We are the creators of our world and outpicture the pure thoughts we dwell on in our consciousness. We see the beauty of a pure consciousness in everyone, the reflection of ourselves. We know about the strength and healing power within everyman. We see the wholeness and perfection in everyone. We draw it forth effectively.

I practice love, the love which I am. In the awareness of the gentle power of my thoughts of love I enter a department store. I see mentally the accomplishment of my shopping. I surround with lovely thoughts: the store, the salesman and the saleswomen. I smile from within and in this radiance I experience kind and skilful assistance from the clerks. I get the size and color of the special clothing I have on my list. Everyone is a practitioner in their own area of activity and in doing their best for others, one does it for himself.

Everyone Is a Practitioner

There is an art in being able *to practice* as being a practitioner. Dr Katarina Suter points this out most charmingly as she uses a child to propound her thesis.

A Child Shall Teach Us

*W*e practice what we believe about ourselves and what we know as true for us in our heart. Everyone practices his **belief** whatever it may be. This is the reason why we are all practitioners.

We ask ourselves: What does the word *practitioner* really mean and how do we express ourselves as a practitioner?

The answer lies in the question. We hear in the word practitioner the word *to practice*. A practitioner is one who practices. The next question is, what do we practice! We practice who and what we are.

We are all here on planet Earth with the same aim. We all choose to be aware of our true nature which is God—the absolute creator—and express (practice) it.

We are an effective practitioner as we consciously practice our choice of being the absolute master of our world through our everyday experience.

I watch a baby in a baby carriage in front of a store. The mother is inside the store doing some shopping. The baby starts to cry. Immediately an older woman stops and goes to the baby rocking it gently in its buggy. The baby keeps on crying. Another woman comes by and takes the baby into her arms, kissing it and speaking gentle words. Now the baby stops crying and thoroughly *enjoys its creation.* The baby knows exactly how to get attention and he gets it. I think: What a wonderful little practitioner this baby is! *Smile!*

We are effective practitioners regardless of our age, our culture, our religion, our descent or origin. We know how to put a cause into motion and get an effect. Our nature is to create the world to our liking. We recognize the baby as a clear example.

We all enjoy a life full of opportunities to demonstrate our skill as a practitioner. We all are the practitioner which we express by our own choice. We are the creator of the experiences through which we demonstrate our mastership. We are all practitioners because we are here for the one and same purpose: To be who we are!

The ease at which we are inclined to give up responsibility for being and doing what we know is correct is rather amazing. Dr Sylvia Maria Enz suggests we are master of our universe and illustrates proof of that contention.

A Master Concept

*W*e are here on planet Earth to find ourself. To find ourself means becoming aware of who and what we really are. We have intrinsically in us the knowingness of our reality. In the measure of our inner readiness we create ourselves on the path to spiritual illumination friends catalyzing in us the awareness of who we really are. Now in our understanding the practitioner is one who knows who we are and acts as a living example to everybody in his world. We demonstrate our belief about ourselves.

With this understanding we say that everyone is a practitioner because everyone demonstrates what he believes. We all outpicture every instant of our life exactly what we believe as true about ourselves. We always demonstrate to ourselves how beneficially we use the Law of cause and effect to bring about the truth in our everyday experiences.

Everyone is the master of his world.

We all choose abundance, health, peace, harmony and other positive virtues as our divine birthright. How do we bring them about in our lives if we experience less than what is our heart's desire for ourselves. We put another cause in motion. We change the acceptance of our consciousness to only the highest and best. We know that we are what we consider good and beautiful and the only thing is to accept it into our experience. We do this by making positive affirmations to ourselves about ourselves. We practice saying the truth.

I have an illustration concerning one little aspect in my life which strengthens me in this concept. I like sneezing. Whenever I feel a tickle in my nose I expect a big joyful sneeze. But in my consciousness I have also built up the idea that sneezing is connected with having a cold. So whenever I feel the tickle in my nose I immediately say to myself: I am whole and perfect. Whenever I hear or see somebody sneezing I immediately say it also. In this way I change the thought into a beneficial one, before I gave an old concept power to manifest. Colds have disappeared from my experience. This is a practitioner's work and reward!

As practitioners we tell ourselves every moment of the day how wonderful we are; how super we are doing. We tell ourselves that we love everybody in our world and that we are loved by everybody. We say that we do all in perfect right action. We are pure, beautiful and good—and so is everybody in our world. We continuously tell ourselves that we have the perfect job, the perfect relationship, the perfect boss and that we are happy, content and in perfect peace. We are unlimited beingness.

As we practice these positive affirmations a change in our consciousness takes place. We do it with discipline, diligence, dedication, determination in the face of every experience telling us the contrary—and all race consciousness fades away. Every selfcreated limitation fades into nothingness. Every positive affirmation is a statement of truth, a new cause.

How we create and see everybody in the light of truth is as we see ourselves. We express the truth in our world. Now we see everybody experiencing his real self. Now we see everybody practicing the truth about themselves as we are living the truth. We now find it easy to put the Law into motion in a beneficial way—and we find it easy

49

Everyone Is a Practitioner

and a great joy to catalyze our friends to the same beneficial use of the Law of cause and effect.

> We are always sharers. We know who we are. We know *who* our creation are. We know the principle upon which all life and action is based. Dr Ilse Wenk reveals how sharing the Law of cause and effect can result in wholeness.

Sharing Wholeness

A practitioner is an absolute sharer of love, understanding and knowingness. Everyone is a sharer. Everyone is a practitioner.

Our practice is to bring to the understanding of ourselves, in those who come to us with healing desires, the Law of cause and effect. Our goal is that everyone use the Law of cause and effect consciously. The Law of cause and effect is the only Law in the universe. Everyone who talks to us is introduced to it. To use the Law wisely is the practitioner's plan for his friends.

A friend came to me with questions on his heart. His mother was ill. He wanted her healthy. I talked with him about the Law of cause and effect. Every thought is a cause and the effect, that means what we experience in our life, equals exactly the thought we have put into motion. When we think a strong thought we have a strong effect, when we think a weak thought we have a weak effect.

I told him that first he treats himself in meditation and sees himself whole and perfect, and then sees his mother whole and perfect. Several weeks later he called me and told me of the miraculous healing of his mother. He said he is so thankful for the talk he had with me. I told him that he is now practicing the Law consciously and that he is a practitioner. Everyone is a practitioner at all times. Our goal is that everyone use the Law of cause and effect consciously.

Practitioners practice love and understanding. Everyone practices love and understanding! Practitioners show all who are interested, how the Law of cause and effect works. The moment we know how the Law of cause and effect works, it is being applied as we apply it, consciously and aware. Therefore I say: Everyone is a practitioner.

The practitioner recognizes his own purity and in so doing recognizes this same purity in everyone he creates in his universe. Dr Robert Rettel lives in his pure mind and claims this unblemished consciousness for all.

All Is Pure

*E*veryone is a practitioner for we the practitioner see in all the pure reflection of ourselves.

We take great care of our thoughts; we watch each thought carefully and completely dwell on thoughts of wholeness, purity and perfection. Our vision is pure; we see our universe with eyes of purity. Our consciousness is filled with purity; all our attention is on purity. Our thinking program is on purity; we think purity, we speak purity, we act with a pure mind. We breathe purity with every breath. We are purity; our world is purity. We know purity; we see purity in all our affairs.

As a practitioner we do one thing: we see everybody from the highest viewpoint—we see all pure, perfect and whole. We use the Law of the universe and put into motion a program of total purity. With this program we experience purity. With this program of purity we bring in our world joy, purity, perfection, wholeness, and abundance. With this program we create our universe as pure and perfect. We fill our world with pure, perfect and whole people. With our eyes we see purity all the time; we are practitioners of the game of life: we practice purity and we see everyone as a practitioner of the game on the same level as we, we see everyone as a practitioner of purity and perfection.

We determine a program of purity for us; we experience absolute purity. Our universe is filled with purity. From our pure thought program we create purity and everyone is pure, everyone is a practitioner of purity as we are.

I speak my word for purity where exists less than perfection, less than purity in a colleague at work. I treat with statements of truth as: *I am pure and perfect.* I see this colleague pure and perfect. I see the work done by him perfectly. I see him at my level, as a practitioner, as a divine center of purity, perfection and love. I see him now as very skilful in many areas; he is gentle and patient with people, he is a fine organizer of his work, he is a skilful initiator of his activities. I discover more and more skills in him; I see goodness and perfection in him, and so it is!

◆

It is so easy to say everyone is a practitioner. Yet to look at the world of our creation reminds us of a battleground. We say to ourselves: we truly are not such good creators.

What we see is only the *game card* which establishes the challenge before us. How do we go about effectively achieving our *dream world* of peace, love, harmony, right action, and *goodness* when we have not purified our own heart and mind, eyes and consciousness, to see reality? The answer is simple: *a journey of 1000 miles begins with the first step,* said Lao-Tse. So our *impossible* journey into fulfilling our real nature of all that is beneficial, begins with one pure thought at a time, one pure vision at a time.

As we label our world so it is.

We may label anything—as we choose to name our children for various reasons—let us label our universe good and beautiful, without judgment let us accept all and call forth all expression to rep-

Everyone Is a Practitioner

resent that which we call beneficial *for ourselves* alone!

We can only love our neighbors as we love ourselves after we determine how we love ourselves. It is an inside, selfchosen, job!

Everyone is a practitioner. We—HOWEVER—are everyone. We create all in our world. We create all fulfilled and fulfilling now! ∞

Theme Three

A PRACTITIONER'S RESPONSIBILITY

*I*t would be so easy to place the burden of guilt upon the shoulders of the friend who comes to the practitioner for wholeness. In doing this the practitioner proves to himself that he is not the creator of his world. Nothing happens by chance in our world.

Hence, every practitioner has created every friend who comes to him for healing. As the practitioner sees the friend, as he sees himself, whole and perfect, the practitioner realizes there is nothing to heal.

The responsibility of the practitioner is to see first himself whole and perfect, then see his creation—friend—whole and perfect. Seeing in this

A Practitioner's Responsibility

manner it is obvious there is nothing left to heal. There is the necessity of maintaining a wholeness balance. The practitioner is the greatest balancer—equalizer—in his universe. He maintains his sight always upon wholeness as his choice.

It does not matter to the practitioner if it appears the friend *wants to be otherwise*, the practitioner can only create after his own image of perfection.

So works the Law according to our choice.

Dr Ellen Jermini defines what it means to be *God* and living up to this expression of perfection to walk the path of life as a magnificent being.

The Business of God

*W*e practitioners have one task in life and this is to mind our own business. This *business* or task is the responsibility of being: being ourselves, God, the allness, the absolute.

What does this mean to us: being God. We know that God is all that God is everywhere and in everything, that God is in, as, and through everything existing. For this reason we too are God, the allness of God, GOD totally!

This is our ONE and only responsibility, being our real self—and acting upon it here on Earth as a divine-human being, recognizing our world as a mirror of ourselves, recognizing God as ourselves in all.

Let us look into the following example: We are a school teacher and teach our students mathematics. We have a class of twenty-two children who each express their individual self. How do we create these children, how do we see these little angels? We see in them exactly that which we create through our thinking, that which we recognize as truth in each child. We see what we are: intelligence, understanding, perception and knowledge. We create the child in our image, the God-image. We create the child as a dedicated, diligent, disciplined, determined student eager to comprehend, excited about learning, a perfect mirror of ourself the teacher. We know that the child knows!

As we speak of responsibility we know our task through the inner voice of our heart. We humbly follow this sweet whispering voice of love and goodness. Intuitively we listen to the first thought which enters our mind and flow with our instinctive self. We are divine, we are God—we are an expression of ourselves: God, the allness!

As practitioners we walk the path of life practicing that what we are. We are what we think we are but, what do we think we are? We are magnificent beings, we are the creator and creation of all, we are all, we are God, we are responsible for what we are.

A Practitioner's Responsibility

We are entirely responsible for our thoughts, words and actions as tools to define our spiritual reality, states Dr Stefan Strässle, as he includes all human functions in the aura of perfection.

Thoughts—Words—Actions: Our Tools

A practitioner's responsibility is equal to his general responsibility in life.

We have created ourselves on planet Earth to remember who we are and to play the game of dwelling in a physical vehicle (our body), of living in a physical world with its illusions of smell, taste, touch, hear and see while being a spiritual entity seeking to return in awareness to the pure essence of all beingness: the allness, oneness, nothingness and isness which is pure spirit!

We have created tools for ourselves with which to practice. These tools are called our thoughts, words and actions.

By thinking our thoughts, by speaking our words and by performing our actions, we practice discipline. Every thought we think, every word we speak and every action we do brings about an effect into our life experience. It brings about a physical manifestation according to the cause we put into motion.

It takes discipline and onepointedness to achieve exactly what we desire. It takes discipline, diligence, determination, dedication and one-

PRACTITIONERS MANUAL

pointedness to think, speak and act in the way we choose for from each seed we plant (thought, word and action) we reap its harvest.

This is our responsibility in life, to discipline ourself in thought, word and deed. This is the only responsibility of a practitioner.

For every thought, word and action the practitioner thinks, speaks and performs he gets an equal effect. As practitioners we always work with our own consciousness. We are only responsible for our own thoughts, words and deeds although we may speak the word about a friend in our life who asks us for prayer or healing treatment. Always it is in our consciousness where the prayer or the treatment takes place. It is the thought we the practitioner have for which we are responsible.

I remember a significant example: My sister Bernadette from Switzerland told me that her doctors said she could never get pregnant and give birth to children.

This was a very limiting report. She was 26 years old and anxious to have children. So she asked me to pray for her. I did so. I visualized her being fertile and mentally saw her happily enjoying life as a mother. Upon returning from another visit with the doctors one month later Bernadette was overwhelmingly happy to tell me that she was pregnant with her first child!

A practitioner's responsibility is to see his world/creation exactly as he sees himself. This of course is always the case for we can only see what we are ourselves within our consciousness. However, we as practitioners see ourselves whole and perfect in body, mind and spirit; we see ourselves as pure, beautiful, joyful, wise, harmonious and prosperous expressing total selflove. The same we see in our creation.

The principle responsibility of a practitioner is to be true to himself, insists Dr Ingeborg Puchert. So as our vision is clear we can only demonstrate in our affairs and that of our friend, our creation, our belief about ourself. Looking at our creation we know what we believe about ourselves.

A Practitioner's High Calling

We know the responsibility a practitioner assumes in training himself for this high calling and accepting the title of practitioner. The principle responsibility of a practitioner is to be true to himself. We know that this title is good for everybody also for those who may live in ignorance of the truth about themselves, for everybody is a practitioner.

We are fully aware of what is the responsibility of a practitioner of the Church of God Unlimited. We know that a practitioner is responsible for the thoughts he has about himself and his world. We know that a practitioner works with the Law of cause and effect. We readily experience the effect of the cause we put in motion mentally or verbally.

We know that the cause we put in motion by our thoughts—by every thought we think—we harvest instantly as the desired effect.

We understand that a practitioner must know and live harmoniously with the principles, the eternal principles governing the existence of everything in the universe. The practitioner has responsibility over whatever he creates for himself and in his world. The practitioner creates everything as a reflection of what he thinks he is.

We see in a practitioner a spiritual healer who takes the responsibility for his thoughts and consciously keeps the state of his mind in perfect balance. The reflection of perfect inner balance he sees is the outpicturing of his beingness. In the state of inner peace of mind the practitioner experiences wholeness and health from within. The practitioner is responsible for recognizing in the friend who calls upon him for guidance or treatment the power of acting by and for himself. We know that a practitioner views the health of the friend and sees it brought forth through the Law by the friend himself for himself.

The practitioner is responsible for recognizing in his own raised consciousness the truth about the friend and sees the friend living the desire of his heart.

Our responsibility is to be a centered, balanced and humble being, declares Dr Katarina Suter. *We are centered as we are onepointed on our pure vision; we are balanced as we are blind to contrary appear-*

ances; and we are humble as we know the Law of cause and effect is supreme and always active.

On Being Centered

*W*e all have responsibilities and each responsibility is selfchosen. However, there is a responsibility which includes all our little and big responsibilities. We as a practitioner are intrinsically aware of this one as the allencompassing responsibility. The responsibility is to know the truth about ourselves and to recognize it in all of our creation. We ask ourselves: what is the truth! The truth is that we are the absolute creator of our world, that we are God and that we see ourselves reflected in all that which we create.

We walk into a room filled with people who are inundated in a loud and aggressive discussion. Here we find a wonderful opportunity to take responsibility and see the truth in our creation. We walk into this room and inwardly speak our word for peace and harmony. We speak our word in our heart for we know that this crowd of hotly discussing people is but a reflection of our own thought. We walk in between the people and share words of love and peace. We direct our attention on harmony and oneness. We point out the positive aspects of the discussion and establish vibrations of constructiveness and unity. We act as a responsible practitioner! We look behind the outer appearance and claim the truth.

Our responsibility is to be a centered, balanced and humble being. In a state of perfect inner balance we are open for the acceptance of the truth about ourselves. Therefore it is important for us to daily meditate and introspect, for in meditation and introspection we are aware of our true nature which is God. In these moments we are absolutely aware of our responsibility. In our daily life we live and express the responsibility which we find in meditation and introspection. We are responsible practitioners for we know the truth about ourselves!

A practitioner asks himself, says Dr Sylvia Maria Enz, what is *the exact thought intent of our original cause (thought)*. Truly, we complain of some of our demonstrations yet what our actual intention of creation is we achieve as an experience in our world. We are held accountable for our thoughts, words and deeds regardless of their outcome. Hence we see purity in all.

We Are Held Accountable

*A*s effective practitioners we are responsible for every thought we think. We are responsible for every experience we create into our world. With every thought we put a cause in motion for the effect we experience. So we are responsible first for the thought we think and for the effect we

A Practitioner's Responsibility

create with it. We take responsibility for our creation as our thought creation.

What does it mean to be responsible for our creation. With every effect we create in our world we experience the manifestation of our thought in the exact thought intent of the original cause (thought). We always find our first thought expressed in every effect and we as practitioners discipline ourselves to keep track of every thought. We may change the cause at any time and we do this very effectively by treating our consciousness to the acceptance of only desirable causes as effects into our daily experience.

We might think: *What if my boss tells me that I have to do a job I dislike to do? The only choice is to do it because I have agreed to do every job I am assigned to do.* This statement is correct but it shows where we did not take charge of our world in the first place. We always get what we expect. Everybody in our world perfectly reflects our thinking and we always get the response we expect. As our thinking is filled with loving thoughts—we experience loving responses. As we expect only beneficial assignments when we are called to the office of the boss: we get them. The Law always works!

We as practitioners live in the awareness of truth. We know who we are. Our main responsibility is to live and to express this truth in every area of our life. We know who we are and as God in its allness we have the responsibility of participating in only desirable and harmonious events. We create in our world only reflections of purity and love. Our responsibility is to accept our real self as reflected by everyone in our world. We live in a world of true magnificence.

As a practitioner we are responsible for ourselves, regales Dr Ilse Wenk. The art and science of wholeness is a precise wisdom used by all knowingly and unknowingly. Dr Wenk suggests we live as an unconditional sharer of love and wisdom we are at all times.

Unconditional Sharer

*W*e are all divine. We are all practitioners. A practitioner is a sharer of love and wisdom. This everyone is and does. Therefore we are all practitioners.

The practitioner's work is being responsible for all his thinking, speaking and doing. We think good thoughts, speak good words and do good actions. As practitioners we are only concerned with our own state of awareness. We treat ourselves in love and wisdom. Whatever we do we do it to perfection. We live our inner life in the art and science of wholeness.

We have no patients but we call all who come to us for guidance friends. It is our responsibility to show the friend the way he can walk it alone through the Law of cause and effect. We do not advise or suggest a specific cause, we just tell the friend all about the Law of cause and effect and

A Practitioner's Responsibility

how the thinking is adjusted to the fact that every thought we think is important and that a thought is a cause.

We tell the friend that first of all we love ourselves thus loving our brothers, our fellowmen. As practitioners we work first of all on our own inner awareness and we take total responsibility for thoughts and words and actions. To be responsible for our life means that we stand up for the principle, that we stand up for all! We can only be responsible for ourselves.

A friend came for some guidance and told me that she lived her life without beneficial cause to herself. She had left her children and her husband to go her own way. I treated myself with all the power of the universe to see her whole and perfect. Then I could see her in the purity and integrity of her beingness and I was happy to see her strong in her choice.

It is most important that the practitioner gives no advice to his friend. A practitioner shows the way into his own inner by regarding and respecting the Law of cause and effect. Every thought which is thought individually is exactly the cause as what happens in our life. As the practitioner we are responsible for ourselves and all our creation—our mirror.

Many times as practitioners we use the term *new* for now. Dr Robert Rettel says: *We thus give a new shape, a new mold to our world. Every thought is a new cause, we create for us a new effect, a new*

result by each thought. While syntactically *new* is a correct word to use, after all whatever is before is new or now. So we know the word *new* as a separate choice we make of total perfection.

New Is Now

*W*e are responsible for our thoughts, words and actions.

As practitioner we are responsible for our thoughts: every thought that we think, every thought that we allow consciously or unconsciously in our mind. We create our universe by every thought that we think. By every thought we put a new cause in motion, by every thought we make the Law work for us, by every thought we present input to the Law. We thus give a new shape, a new mold to our world. Every thought is a new cause; we create for us a new effect, a new result by each thought.

We determine to keep our thoughts pure, to keep our thoughts all the time on a high vantage point: on the spiritual reality that we are, on the indwelling divinity. By this decision we put the beneficial cause in motion for us and our world. We continue with this pure thought program as we watch our thoughts and allow pure, positive thoughts in our consciousness. We dwell in beauty, in harmony, in goodness, in peace, in wholeness. We think of whole and perfect bodies and minds; we think all day long of perfection.

A Practitioner's Responsibility

That is the thought program we keep foremost all the time in our mind. We think of the divinity that we are; we think of ways and manners for expressing more of our Godself.

We keep our thoughts pure; we dwell all the time in our inherent, our innate purity and we speak thus only pure words, words in accord with our divine nature, and we perform only pure acts, by which we reveal and express beautifully our Godself.

We are responsible for our thoughts, our words and our acts and we take total responsibility for our thoughts, words and acts.

I take responsibility for my thoughts at work; during my work I watch my thoughts. Every second I take time—and direct all my thinking in a positive, beneficial way for me. During the day I think of the spiritual reality that I am, and sing in my heart: I am God, God I am. And I experience that what I think of: beauty, joy, peace and harmony with all the people in my world.

◆

Most people like to say that others are responsible for their lives and that the entire world dictates whatever it is that they experience. This has been taught to us by our parents, our peers, and our friends. Historically we have been bound by these assumptions. Strangely, we seem to enjoy this condition.

As a practitioner, we have no excuse to continue in this avenue of thinking. All the world is our mirror. Whatever we are thinking within ourselves, this is exactly what is mirrored back to us from the world we have created about us.

On a common level we can recognize that when we are happy, we see happy people; when we are sad, we see sad people. When we walk into a room and enter into the feelings of the people therein, we are pawns of life. When we walk into a room and see a condition for a moment which is not acceptable to us, and then decide to put a new cause into motion, this is what it is all about. We decide to have the room happy, to have the people there responsive to all the harmony and happiness which is our innate beingness.

True, we are the practitioner. At all times we are the practitioner. However, as much as we are the practitioner, so is the friend with whom we work. He is the practitioner of his own life and affairs. While we see him in all his nobility and perfection, we see him fulfilled to his heart's desire, the desire and nobility must be harmonious with our consciousness. We can only create others as we are in ourselves. We are the center of our universe, the pivotal point of our world. All revolves about us. All is from the center which we are. Thus, it is vitally important that we maintain the highest standards for our own personal lives and our own personal convictions.

All the world about us responds to who and what we are. The world about us is our thought, our reflection, our action in reaction.

A Practitioner's Responsibility

The practitioner has a great responsibility to be himself. A practitioner has a great responsibility to recognize what his own thoughts are and to work in harmony with his own reality.

The joy in carrying out this responsibility is beyond measure. It is the bliss the Hindu seeks, it is the heaven the Christian desires most heartily, it is the ultimate reality.

It is our work as a responsible practitioner. ∞

Theme Four

A PRACTITIONER'S PRAYER

To a practitioner prayer is communication with/as God.

Understanding this concept is absolutely necessary for effective practitioner work. For in this concept lies the realization of who we are and who God is—without this knowledge we are working ineffectively and our accomplishments are void of any real impact in a foreseeable way.

To say communication with/as God presumes knowledge of just what the words *with* and *as* signify. To be *with* anything indicates a duality. To be *as* anything means that which the thing is that which is *as* it is. As two drops of water may be with one another, to be as one another defines them quite differently. So it is incumbent upon a

A Practitioner's Prayer

practitioner to know his terminology in the utilization of words, and with the definition of terms.

Would that every practitioner were able to communicate with other people as well as he can communicate with/as God.

First understood must be that the practitioner and God are one. The image we have of God is the absolute, infinite, everywhere present, all powerful, and not in the slightest contained in a personalization, a person, a being, as we know beings. Understanding this we come to realize that the omnipresence of God is in us as us. We are working with a concept, a reality which indeed is ourselves.

The second realization is that those who come to us as practitioners, are our reflection—hence the statement: PHYSICIAN HEAL THYSELF or PRACTITIONER HEAL THYSELF. For when our consciousness is in right order our creation, mankind about us, is in perfect harmony with our perfect design for it.

A practitioner's prayer is pure awareness that whatever it chooses to have done—is done!

Everyone we meet, we meet as our creation, Dr Ellen Jermini insists. All of the power of the universe responds to our creative word and accomplishes our choice. Professor Jermini boldly insists: *Our word is our bond.* Miracles follow.

Our Prayer Fulfills Our Intent

A practitioner lives with the motto: *My word is my bond.* We practitioners understand that indeed our word, each word which we speak, is a powerful prayer, a powerful effect with its appropriate impact in our life. In fact, our thoughts, our words, our deeds are our everlasting prayers. For this reason we say, we live in a constant state of prayer. We live in the silence of our peaceful minded beingness. We live in our introspective self, we pray constantly.

How do we understand this: for example—we visit someone in hospital. As we enter this building, we enter in awe and dignity to ourselves. We realize the temple of the living God, our own body, our total selves as perfection and purity, as love and light and see our environment illumined, recognizing excellence and brilliance radiating out of any corner. We live in the awareness, in the prayer of and to ourselves the one creator, knowing ourselves the allness, GOD, the omniscience, the omnipotence, the omnipower. So whomever we meet *as our creation* in a hospital, we create them as a reflection of ourselves, as an answer to our prayer.

We may ask ourselves why we have created ourselves in such an environment. The answer lies in the question and it flows out of our heart. We are the masters of our creation. Whatever we create for whatever purpose or in the appearance of purposelessness, is good and very good. It is the fulfillment of our prayer, our word, our every moment thought. We are concentrated on our prayer

A Practitioner's Prayer

of the wholeness and the perfection we are as a divine-human being, living here on planet Earth in love to ourselves. We confirm the truth about ourselves, and live nonjudgmentally in the realm of our beingness.

Our word is our bond, it is a powerful prayer, it is an eternal, holy act, it is the revelation of our existence.

Practitioner Dr Stefan Strässle insists that since God indwells each being a practitioner prays within himself—solely! Fulfilling this premise an effective practitioner achieves unimaginable results through the use of the principle.

We Pray To Ourselves

*A*s a practitioner we always pray to ourselves. We pray to our own consciousness. As practitioners we pray for, to and with ourselves solely.

As practitioners we are always in control. We take full responsibility for the world that we create. We take charge of the people therein, the circumstances and conditions, which allow us to be the absolute masters, now and always.

As practitioners we pray to the divine self within us. To pray to the divine self within us means that we see a thought picture, an idea, a new cause, fulfilled right now. As practitioners we positively visualize the solution. Mentally we establish the thought picture of the experience we choose to have. As practitioners we speak our word and see it done.

To pray means that we *accept* and *claim* what we choose to create for ourselves. We remain onepointed. We allow only positive, affirmative, supportive and powerful causes into our consciousness which correspond with the fulfillment of the cause put into motion in the first place.

To demonstrate onepointedness in the solution, we practice discipline. For example: we take each chore—which we create for ourselves—and perform the work as a perfectionist. Doing this is the key to perfect thinking, which is the key to live an illumined life, which is the key to perfect relationships and absolute harmony in business and family life; it is the key to peace, joy, love, happiness and perfect health.

Other virtues which are important to demonstrate onepointedness: diligence, dedication and determination. Through these great ideas and concepts, we practice discipline/onepointedness in a little different way. Through diligence, we practice remaining with a program and never to give in *BUT* come out the winner. Practicing dedication is the wonderful way to learn patience, devotion and joy which we apply in our treatments, meditations and introspective studies. With determination we refer to being determined to an idea or thought. We determine a goal and strive for it onepointedly. All of these new virtues are important to the prayer work of a practitioner.

A Practitioner's Prayer

With her usual mathematical precision practitioner Dr Ingeborg Puchert presents a view of a practitioner's prayer as one which is already accomplished. She points out the creator and the created are one and fulfilled in the isness.

The Powerhouse of the Universe

*W*e know the word prayer and the meaning of it. We say we pray to ourselves for something. We know that we are God, the allness and the only one we call upon is ourselves. We live in the knowingness that everything is within us. The center of universal energy is right within us and we generate it and work with it through the thoughts we have about ourselves.

The practitioner uses the word treatment. Treatment is the powerful affirmation of a state, a specific condition in his life, in his world. The practitioner experiences everything he claims into appearance. The practitioner puts into motion the Law of cause and effect. In the treatment the practitioner affirms onepointedly the effect he chooses and sees in his world.

The practitioner treats out of the knowingness that he is one, he is one as all, he is the oneness himself. The practitioner lives and experiences the existence of everything in the state of isness. He knowingly affirms that everything that there is, just is and is now and forevermore.

The practitioner knows and sees himself **as the creator and the created** of every circumstance in his life. He believes one hundred percent in himself. Out of the state of isness he visualizes everything in manifestation. The practitioner bases his treatment on the conviction that everything he treats for is manifest in his world.

The practitioner loves himself, everybody and everything. The practitioner calls everything good and very good and indeed sees the reality, the truth about everybody and everything.

The practitioner lives totally in the first person, knows only positive expressions in the present tense, the now. Every thought of perfection, wholeness, abundance, health, harmony and right action the practitioner thinks is a treatment; every word he speaks is a treatment. Every achievement is the fulfillment of a desire.

The practitioner keeps his mind, the powerhouse of the universe, pure. The practitioner lives the truth and insists on the truth he affirms about himself and expresses the divine from within himself.

The utilization of a practitioner's prayer work comes alive in the skilful words of Dr Katarina Suter as she defines that whatever and wherever our thought is there is our experience since all in our lives is the creation of our thought. Utilizing the white light of love she defines a new breed of hospital.

A Practitioner's Prayer

We Are the Power of Our Prayers

A practitioner's prayer is the prayer to ourselves. We pray to God within, to the reality of our being. We ask ourselves: what are prayers and what do we pray for?

We create the necessity of a minor surgery on our body. We sit in the hospital waiting room and prepare ourselves for the new experience. We feel a certain uneasiness within us and we know that it is because of the adventure in the hospital. As a practitioner we know the power of prayers; we know that *wherever our thought is, there is our experience.* We put all our attention—heart feelings— in our prayers. We affirm: We are whole and perfect; every organ, action and function of our body is in perfect harmony; we are absolutely relaxed and composed; we are the white light of love and wherever we put our attention there is light and love. We see each being in the hospital waiting room as a master, joyously aware of his choice. We visualize each doctor as an absolute master in his work. We fill ourselves with positive prayer statements and are the master of the situation.

We fill the hospital with positive thoughts and peaceful vibrations through our prayers. We establish the experience in our own image, the image we have about ourselves. We affirm the reality of our being through onepointed prayers. We call this action a prayer, an affirmation, or a treatment. The name sounds different—the action is the same.

We pray to ourselves only for we know that the world is the *creation of our thought*. We are aware of our oneness as all and know that a prayer for ourselves is reflected in all its details in our world. We are aware of the power of our prayers, for they are the building stones of our experience. What a great tool is our prayers!

It is so easy to allow conditions to remain as they are in the world. However a practitioner decides what his world is and what his world expresses and puts the causes in motion to bring about this effect. A hearty working practitioner, Dr Sylvia Maria Enz, defines the work done by a practitioner as acceptance of the truth about ourselves. She insists: Prayer is the acceptance of the reality behind every appearance.

Prayer:
Communication from Self to Self

We as practitioner know who we are and that we are here in this life experience to live our reality. We know we are God and we are God in its allness. In this allness we are all, we know all and are everywhere present.

The experience on this dimension is the adventure of becoming aware of our true self. So

A Practitioner's Prayer

whenever our awareness needs confirmation we turn within and claim the truth about ourselves. We may call this turning within meditation, treatment or prayer. Always it is turning to our source, to our very being.

Prayer is the acceptance of truth in our daily expression.

Prayer is the acceptance of the reality behind every appearance.

We pray for many things: for good health, a loving relationship, for abundance in material goods, or for illumination in the ultimate awareness. Always we turn within to confirm and affirm in being what is already there, what is already accomplished.

We in our allness determine what we manifest out of the infinite storehouse of our existence. Whatever our heart's desire is, we claim and accept it as a fact in our world of experience.

Prayer is this communication from Self to self.

We keep our thoughts/prayers onepointedly on the ultimate truth of our being and everything we experience in our appearance world falls into place in perfect right action.

We at the Absolute Monastery bless our world, the buildings, the animals, the property, all, by visualizing all as the pure white light of love that we are. We see ourselves always as this white light of love and enter the perfect peace of our spiritual reality. It works!

We had mice in the Absolute Monastery pantry. Upon discovery of this fact one of the monks during the blessing times went both in the morning and the evening to the pantry and visualized it in the white light of love and the next day the mice had disappeared.

This is true for all of our life. We as practitioner look at the world of our creation from the awareness of truth. We see all in the white light of love and with this affirmation we accept the one and the all of our being in, as and through everything. The statement of the white light of love is a very powerful one as it puts us immediately in harmony with our spiritual reality.

We are the light; we are the truth; we live the awareness of light; we are the way of the light as we are it always—whatever we do, wherever we are in this world of appearances.

World traveler and linguist Dr Ilse Wenk has met and worked with people from all walks of life who have bent her ear with their tales of insufficiency to be able to accomplish the desire of their heart. Practitioner Wenk guides the *friend* to intelligently state the question of their desire, therein finding the answer (for the answer to any question lies in the question well asked) and then utilizing that answer as the foundation for their positive prayer affirmation as already accomplished—it is accomplished.

A Practitioner's Prayer

A Prayer of Recognition

A practitioner meditates and prays constantly. It is a prayer of better understanding and higher awareness. It is a **prayer of love.**

We include in our daily prayers all our beloveds. We see all our beloveds in the pure white light of love. Our prayer is filled with love and joy of fulfillment.

First we pray a prayer of recognition of the love and happiness in ourselves. Only when we love ourselves are we able to love our friends and our neighbors. Then we think of all our friends (our creation) and include them in our prayer. Actually all our life is a prayer. We think introspectively and deeply in every aspect of our life.

As a practitioner we work together with our beautiful friend. He was not happy about some circumstances in his life. He came to us with his questions and we talked as long as he chose to find the answers to his questions himself. This is because in every question is already the answer.

And a practitioner does not help a friend he only guides his friend with love to the understanding that all is good and very good and that the friend puts a new cause into motion himself. That means that everyone causes everything in his life through his own thought. Every thought is a cause. And according to the only Law there is, the Law of cause and effect we cause the thought to go in the direction we choose. Hence we are responsible.

Our friend is very happy as we pray and has the result of love, joy and happiness according to our prayer.

Prayer is communion as God. In the silence of our inner we communicate with our inner in the language of God. This means our praying word of love, light, understanding, right action, and happiness. Prayer is not to beg but to be one as God. When we are praying the feeling comes in our communication of being God and good.

Prayer is a very private affair. Therefore effective prayer is not done in public. We are the God presence within and talk in divine wisdom with our inner and get all the answers for which we ask.

Prayer is the most beautiful communion of the soul with the heart. The practitioner's prayer always includes all his friends who come for guidance to him as the practitioner. All life is a prayer. A deep communion as God.

Knowing that perfection exists eternally and everywhere the practitioner has a unique task of working with himself and his *friends* to see that which is ever present. Just as a cloud hides the valley below the mountain top, the valley is at all times present in all its reality. So Dr Robert Rettel defines that the prayer of the practitioner reveals that which is there all the time.

A Practitioner's Prayer

Recognize Perfection
Already Present in Our World

*A*s practitioners we pray and treat to recognize the manifestation of perfection already a reality in our universe for ourselves and for all the people in our universe.

When we pray, we claim the truth: we are whole and perfect since the very beginning; our entire universe is whole and perfect since the beginning. We claim our divine birthright, which is ours since the beginning. Our good is there for us, but we experience it as we claim it.

We claim our good with a conscious conviction that it is our divine birthright, that it is ours right now. We pray, we treat to see the manifestation of perfection: we recognize that perfection is already in our world, we establish this perfection by statements of truth; we visualize our world as absolutely perfect right now.

We are aware that it is our divine birthright to experience this total wholeness and perfection. It is up to us to claim that which is ours. We get only as much as we can take, we get according to our belief, according to our innermost convictions.

Prayer is an inner *activity*. We address the prayer, the treatment to the inner presence, to the inner divinity. We recognize that we enjoy our good ourselves by our thoughts, our convictions, our beliefs, our expectations. We expect the best and the very best for us, we think highly of us and we experience the very best. Our thoughts all the time are on perfection, on purity, on wholeness; we have in our world absolute perfection by these positive thoughts.

We address our prayers and our treatments to ourselves. We speak the truth about ourselves, we think the truth about ourselves. A prayer is a communication as ourselves.

In our quiet moments we recognize God within us as the source of all our good; we recognize God as the supply of all our good. A prayer is a communication as the indwelling divinity.

I recognize as the *highest* prayer, the highest treatment, the absolute truth about myself: I am God. I pray all day long, I treat all day long: I live in awareness as the indwelling, divine presence. I consciously make contact as God in me by stating that I am one as God and I sing in my heart: I am God, God I am.

◆

The most significant work done by any practitioner in his prayer treatment with his creation and hence primarily with himself is the recognition that all that is *desired* is already present, fulfilled, manifest and being enjoyed by everyone who has the vision to see the truth.

Each of the practitioners in this volume work daily with hundreds of beings around the globe. They are in the Swiss mountains, the united Germany, the outback of Australia, the sunny Califor-

A Practitioner's Prayer

nia foothills, the reaches of every hamlet and village in America, South America, England and every land on our Earth—each working nobly with their creation defining and redefining the ever present reality that each is God and each is both the created and the creator.

Understanding a practitioner's prayer is tremendously important to fulfilling humanity's purpose of existence. This purpose is the recognition that nothing new can ever be created for everything is.

Once this reality is assimilated by all, all know abundance, perfection and harmony.

For this we share our reality. ∞

Theme Five

THE PRACTITIONER
THE CREATOR

*W*e have been taught all of our lives that we are the microcosm of the macrocosm, we are a child of the universe, that at all times there is something bigger than we are. With this type of thinking we continually believe that we are but pawns in the great chess game of life.

All great philosophers and religious teachers insist that the overall being which is the essence of all life is in and through all of its creation as itself; and that which the infinite is the finite is and the finite remains finite until such time as it recognizes that it at all times is and was the infinite.

The magnificent intelligence of the universe which demonstrates itself in and through us as us is neither belittled nor enlarged by our acceptance of who and what we are. It just is; we just are; all just is—ONE!

From this point of view, insofar as all is one, and we are the creator of all in our experience, we know no otherness, we know no persons, places or things outside of ourselves—we are all. All we see is but a reflection of what we think about ourselves and about that which we create.

The possibility of being either human or divine is the perspective given to us by Dr Ellen Jermini as she reveals that all we do during our Earth experience is to have fun, creating all for the purpose of fulfilling our dynamic imagination. She shows the process to enjoy beneficial creation by first knowing what it is that we would like to create.

Beneficial Creating

*W*e practitioners create our world through our thought—everyone does and therefore everyone is a practitioner—a creator. We create ourselves as divine-human beings to live here on planet Earth and to have fun in, as, with our creation. We are the creator and the creation as we are the thinker and the thought and in oneness of our beingness we bring forth any desire of our heart. We know who we are—GOD, total power and we use this power as the absolute creator, being disciplined, dedicated, determined, and diligent.

What does a practitioner create?

We practitioners create our body which is our tool in which to practice. We practice positive thinking and practice the use of the universal Law, the LAW OF CAUSE AND EFFECT. As we think our thought—in oneness with the LAW, the Law manifests our thought—so we create.

So we often create ourselves in the wonderful mountains of Switzerland. We enjoy a lovely winter in the snow covered alps. We create a warm, sunny day, a great day to ski. We love the light movements of our body and smoothly follow our skis gliding perfectly down the mountain. We take charge of every movement, turning to the right, to the left as it is our joy and pleasure. We have fun and are absolutely aware of what we do. However, we have the choice, the choice to finish our day in glory and triumph at home or to create ourselves in the glory of a hospital—creating the experience of a broken leg.

The Law of cause and effect brings forth any thought, the thought of a perfect leg, the thought of a perfectly broken leg. It is up to us—as practitioners, as master-creators—to create wisely, beneficially, to fulfill our heart's desire.

As practitioners we know our birthright, we know our home, we know the reality of our being, we know the truth about ourselves. We live in this reality domain. We are GOD, the absolute creator of our world and in this awareness we create without judgment, we create our world absolutely perfect and we call it good, very good.

Medical wonders are normal occurrences when we effectively and properly use the Law of cause and effect, points out Dr Stefan Strässle. When we as practitioners onepointedly use the Law by placing causes we wish to express into action, effects equal to our causes manifest. It is the nature of the Law to perform upon our request exactly as our request is made.

LAW: nonjudgmental, unconditional, affirmative

*A*s practitioners we are the absolute creator. We are totally in charge of our life and affairs.

This is true since first of all we are the practitioner, and second we create our world by our thoughts, words and actions. We work with the Law of cause and effect, the one eternal Law of the universe.

The nature of the Law is to be nonjudgmental, unconditional and affirmative. The Law works at all times, under all circumstances. We activate the Law by the thoughts we think, the words we speak and the actions we perform. Essentially we can even say that it is **only our thoughts** which create our life's experiences for it is the thought itself which brings forth the word we speak and the action we do.

We as practitioners know the Law and use it wisely. That means, we consciously and knowingly think our thoughts for as it is: every thought brings about an effect. We can experience whatever we choose to. We are absolutely free and limitless.

As practitioners we create our world beautifully and positively. That means that everything and everybody in our world is beautiful and positive. To experience this state of consciousness, we think beautiful and positive thoughts.

We as practitioners always conceive of beautiful and positive attitudes, in each moment, in whatever circumstances we find ourselves. This is the *clue* to be absolutely in control of our life. By being positive and by thinking beautiful and uplifting thoughts, we always come out the winner.

To illustrate the power of positive thinking is the magnificent story of a Swiss lady, my sister Bernadette. Bernadette was six months pregnant and the doctor told her that she would have to give birth to her second child through a Caesarean operation. My sister, being quite excited and nervous, asked me to pray for her. A few days later she had another visit with her doctor. He could not believe his eyes. He found that the infant had miraculously turned in the womb (a medical wonder) and now lay in the perfect position so that his mother was able to give birth in the normal way which she did and Mirjam was born.

The Practitioner the Creator

It is always when we as practitioners speak positive, beautiful and uplifting prayers that wondrous results take place.

Dr Ingeborg Puchert points out that professional practitioners live in a constant state of meditation, a metaphysical treatment. Doing this is the same as breathing. Carefully husbanding every thought, word and deed results in an accomplished practitioner.

Professional Practitioners

We are practitioners and practice what we believe we are. We give the very best of ourselves to ourselves in our specialty, the area of metaphysical treatment. We are professional practitioners and practice this spiritual ability in our daily life and activities. We experience the effect of what we think about ourselves as we apply the teaching of positive thinking.

We carefully watch the thoughts we entertain about ourselves in our consciousness. We look behind the appearances and see the divine reality in our creation—everything and in everybody.

The physical body is the exchangeable coat in which we wrap our spiritual reality. We are God, we are the allness. We accept and proclaim our spiritual invulnerability. We delight in looking at a feature of our body and define it with the words beautiful, perfect, eternal, vital and invulnerable.

We practitioners and ministers of the Church of God Unlimited are in the state of meditation all day long. We are active in preaching the divine presence and healing power. We have a positive attitude about the relative world about us. We live in the relative world and are true to our real world, the spiritual one.

We are the living example of the indwelling God presence. We rightfully call our physical body the temple of the living God. We love and respect this human yet divine vehicle, a vehicle of perfection, the perfection we are.

We have within us the allknowingness and practice it. The answer to whatever question we have, we reveal from within. The answer we find in the question itself.

We listen to the divine within us. We live in the knowingness of our real being. And out of the inner knowing, the omniscience, we accept the role of creator in the game of life here on planet Earth. Indeed this is the truth about ourselves. We live up to this everlasting truth.

We are the omnipotence of the universe and apply it in the activity of creation from within.

We create ourselves as omnipresent beings. In this state of omnipresence we are everywhere. We mentally create ourselves in the place where our *friends* live. We mentally join those for whom we treat in the knowingness that we are they.

The Practitioner the Creator

In innocent recognition is the power of the Law of cause and effect to issue forth our edict. The Law's purpose is but to produce our request. Dr Katarina Suter directs our attention to the effective manifestation of the principle. The Law, says Dr Suter, is but a tool which we learn to use. Herein she shows its simple and effectual use.

Blue Sky on Command

*W*e as trained practitioners have a unique tool at our disposition—we call it the Law of cause and effect. The Law of cause and effect is the one Law with which we create our world. The Law of cause and effect is used by us every instant of our life—consciously or unconsciously. Our task as effective practitioners/creators is to use the Law consciously! Our responsibility is to be aware of each cause we *put* into motion. With this awareness we create our world.

We awaken and look out of the window. We see a rainy overcast sky. Our choice is to experience a blue sky and wonderful sunshine! As a practitioner and the creator of our world we immediately speak our word for a blue sky and sunshine. Onepointedly we put the cause of blue sky and sunshine into motion and experience the effect. We look out of the window and see our cause manifested. We are without astonishment about the manifestation of the blue sky and sunshine for we know that whatever we see in our world is OUR creation.

As the creator we take responsibility for each experience in our life for we know that it is our thought which brings the experience about. As the creator we know that we are the center of our world and the source of all existence. The seed for any experience we choose to have slumbers within our own being. Through our onepointed thought we bring the experience into existence.

As conscious creators we train ourselves in onepointedness and discipline. These are the essential qualities of an effective creator. We discipline our mind to have one thought at a time and bring it into existence. The effect is the proof of our onepointed and disciplined thought.

As a practitioner and creator of our world we know that the physical experience is the illusion. Behind each illusion we find the reality which is the thought. We are free to create whatever we choose, however we choose and whenever we choose. We are unlimited creators for we are our own source.

With harmonious simplicity Dr Sylvia Maria Enz illustrates the fact that from the little to the large, nothing is too big or small for our specific use of the principle to achieve our choice. So we might as well create loving illusions.

Creation Is Our Choice Manifested

What a lovely topic. What infinite possibilities await us as the practitioners of our world. We have come to this planet Earth into this life experience to create it in our image and to enjoy what we create. We know who we are and with this awareness we consciously create our world.

The world is our playground to expand and to apply our creative imaginative genius from within into outward expression. We as practitioners have a clear picture of our world. We know what is harmonious and most beneficial for us—and so we visualize, we think our world into being.

We know the truth and so we understand that all is perfect as it is. We see beyond the appearance. We choose to live in a world of illusions—so we might as well create beneficial, lovely illusions in our experience.

Creation is our choice manifested.

We are the creator of every experience in our life. We all are confronted day by day by experiences like the woman who went to the supermarket and while counting fruit into a bag observed the following scene: Next to her an employee is filling in fruit on a stand. A customer asks a question in a rather unfriendly way. He gets a short impersonal answer. From the other side another customer approaches with a smile and with a very joyful voice asks information. The employee turns to this patron and in the same joyful way answers the request of the man. Watching this last scene the woman thinks that this is like looking into the bright light of the sun on a lovely summer day. We are the creators of our world and the world of creation is our reflection.

Or like the woman calling the healing ministry asking: *Why is it that everybody in my world denies me? I have always acted correctly toward them!* She gets the answer: *Nobody in your world denies you but yourself.*

It is always our choice how our world responds to our creative expectation. Creation begins in ourselves, peace begins in ourselves, love begins in ourselves. We as practitioners know the truth about ourselves and our world and live in the constant reflection of love and peace. Our world outpictures what we are: Love, peace, abundance, health, joy and harmony in all our actions.

Evidence of our being creators of our world shines forth through the words of Dr Ilse Wenk as she demonstrates how through our charisma we create *others*, as we call them *friends*, who seemingly need us and want to be in our charisma, our reflected light! In our little game of life we pretend that the *friend* does not know what it truly wants to experience and with our professional knowing we proddingly encourage the *friend* to find the answer in themselves—ourselves.

The Practitioner Has Charisma

The role of the practitioner is being the creator. We take total responsibility for our thought, word and deed. The practitioner brings about a world wonderfully joyous, beautiful.

We as practitioners create our world through our charisma. Our main activity is love. Love for our world and for our universe and all we people it with.

A *friend* came to us for help. He had a list of questions in his hand when he started talking. We went through all the items until—amazingly—our *friend* found all answers for himself. We are the creator of our world. We create a world of knowing and understanding.

As the creator we are omniscient, omnipresent and omnipotent. We create a world of love. We create a world of understanding and happiness. We create a world of joy and light. All want to be near us because it is so beautiful to be in our world as we create it. The world we create is a world of harmony and peace. Every thought we think is a thought of peace and love.

When a *friend* comes to us we talk with him about the Law of cause and effect. The Law of cause and effect is the only universal Law. We talk with the *friend* about the thought that every thought is most important. When the *friend* comes with a problem we talk to him about how he can put a new cause into motion. We tell the *friend* that every thought brings about an effect which is equal exactly to the cause we put into motion through our thought. We just guide. We let the *friend* find the new cause himself. We are good creators. We think good thoughts, speak good words and do good deeds.

We as practitioners are the creators of our world in a very special way. First we create our consciousness in the state of absolute purity and integrity. We meditate and give our love to our *friends* with all our heart and all our soul.

We practitioners are the creators of love and joy, happiness and understanding, and practice discipline, dedication, determination, onepointedness and humility and share this all with our *friends*.

Being an effective practitioner demands we take time during every day to center our attention in our divine nature and draw this forth into expression by our attention to it, says Dr Robert Rettel. Using the theater as his example, Practitioner Rettel illustrates the many roles we effectively play innumerable times daily in our lives.

Every Practitioner a Thespian

*W*e are the creator of our world. By every thought we think, by every word we speak, we actuate the Law and bring a result in our world.

The Practitioner the Creator

We think a thought, we put a cause in motion and we get a result in accord with the cause that we have put in motion.

We create the world in which we live by our choice. We choose our thoughts and words. By this choice we put causes in motion and we select our world. We create every condition, every situation. We are the director in this life game; we direct the events by our thoughts; we create people in our life, in our world by our thought. As the director we decide upon the setting of the stage, upon the costumes worn by the actors; we direct the actors, we instruct the cameramen, we control the play and all events by our commands. We are the creator of the film.

The world is our stage on which we act. We create our entire world by our orders. We think a thought be it ever so tiny and we cause the Law to bring about that result in our world.

As practitioners we are very efficient and very wise directors. We direct our life from the highest vantage point. We control our world from the highest viewpoint. We know who and what we are. We always think, speak and act from the divine center in us; we always put the right cause in motion for us and for our entire universe.

As practitioners we create a beautiful, harmonious, peaceful, wondrous, abundant world filled with love. In our world we create people in accord with what we are: whole and perfect, and loving. We create a world where we give God the priority; we create a magnificent, divine world; we create heaven here on this planet, right now. That is our role as practitioner.

I create a simple, peaceful, harmonious, abundant and divine life. During the day I take my time, I interrupt my activity, and speak my word for divine right action. I close my eyes for some moments and I think peace, harmony and abundance. When I resume my work, I am in a peaceful state, I am in harmony with myself. I continue my work in absolute harmony. I experience total peace and harmony.

◆

In defining the practitioner as the creator, our professional practitioners have revealed sides of their nature which are inherent in all of us.

With each door opening illustration given in this chapter, more are inspired in our thinking from our own daily experiences.

The ability to recognize that as creators we are playing an infinite variety of roles on the stage of life. We are professional thespians and our acting career hinges its successful accomplishment on how well we perform. If we have a sub role of the starring place in the drama/comedy, it does not matter, we give it our very best. For if we choose to be supporting actors as we might in our work as practitioners with our creation, how well we appear as mentors/sharers/teachers depends upon what we foresee the outcome to be.

Being the creator of our world is a tremendous responsibility when viewed in earthly or human

The Practitioner the Creator

terms. When viewed in the reality domain, it is just an isness.

For us, as professional practitioners, we create our world meaningfully on the basis of the values we have established for ourselves.

It is not a matter of right or wrong.

Fulfilling the role of practitioner, or creator, merely means that we DO accomplish our stated goal via our specifically chosen route. So if we choose to play the devil—then we do it magnificently. If we choose to play an angel—we do it magnificently. The *test* for us is how well we have played the game of being a human by the rules which we have placed on our humanness!

This is a very significant concept if we are willing to recognize it. ∞

Theme Six

THE PRACTITIONER'S PRINCIPLE

The practitioner's principle is his primary source of life—the foundation upon which he bases every thought, word and deed. The practitioner knows that his is the world which he has created. The practitioner knows that his is a world that has no values. The practitioner's world has no right or wrong. The practitioner's world is not judgmental, conditional or rational. The practitioner knows that his world just is—hence he must carefully consider all the ramifications of his choices in exercising the Law of cause and effect.

While there is no moralism in any work a practitioner does, so there is no moralism in a priest taking confession or a minister offering sanctuary to a condemned criminal, the work they do just is without judgment. Principle knows no bounds for it is limitless in its profusion of givingness—either *good* or *bad!*

The practitioner (which by the nature of the title and name itself includes all of our creation, animate or inanimate) practices whatever it is he believes about himself and demonstrates in his objective (and subjective) world the fullness of that belief. Often we choose to use the word KNOW rather than BELIEF because know signifies a truism while belief signifies that which is hoped for and sought after but not truly known. We can use belief in our practitioner work because we are working with fledgling ideas and concepts which have not yet gained the real foundation within our consciousness. Once the base is set what formerly was but a belief reveals itself as a knowingness—eternally established as it has always been.

The subjective illustration which Dr Ellen Jermini gives us here in the choice of using alcohol or not is quite common to humanity. The addiction could relate to coffee, tea, cigarettes, drugs, any NEED humanity may have—we may have—even to the need for love from another whom we create not giving it to us; the need for specific foods; the need for relationships; the need for anything in the *outer*; the need for anything in the *inner!* All possess us and the principle confirms to us that this need is binding. The principle also confirms to us, should we so choose, that the former need is no longer binding.

To Drink or Not to Drink

We practitioners have one principle and this is to live in truth to ourselves, clear and alert to our God nature, our real self. We know that we are the creators of our world—we create by our own thoughts, our own words and deeds and this is our integrity, the honesty of our life principle.

We look at the world's heroes, champions or great winners and recognize their outstanding actions in being disciplined, dedicated, diligent and determined on their goal of life. We know with onepointedness in our thinking we achieve any goal we determine as our heart's desire. We set up our rules of life and stand up for whatever we define right and good for ourselves.

For example if we determine for ourselves to avoid alcohol for a certain period of time and choose to drink water, milk or juices, we live up to our choice, our principle. The world may ask us and insist on us to participate in their game of life yet we know that for which we stand, **we respect our word to *ourselves.***

So we are invited to a great birthday party where beer, wine and juices are offered to the guests. We make our choice of beverage. However, we enjoy the juice without any need or want for something else.

The Practitioner's Principle

We practitioners love our selfcreated world; we love our world as we love ourselves. We know that love turns the world around and that this selflove, the love and respect to ourselves, is the key of a happy, fulfilled life, a wonderful life of a master. We are practitioners, we are responsible for using the rules of the games of life. The rules are to be aware of our every thought, word and deed and to know that we alone are the source of health, wealth and goodness, the gold mine of a rich life. We are the presence of God, we are spirit, we are the reality of our life. We stand up for principle, we stand up for that what is right for us alone.

The ability to be at peace within ourselves is one of the first and cardinal rules for any successful practitioner. Dr Stefan Strässle points out that the convictions of a practitioner remain untouched at the center of his consciousness at the center of his awareness—the center of his being. Hence there the practitioner finds the principle upon which he bases his every thought and action.

Our Friend, Our Creation

$\mathcal{T}$he main principle for us as practitioners while practicing our beliefs and convictions is to ALWAYS return to our own conscious awareness, the center of our being.

As practitioners we view our life and experiences from the inner center of harmony, love, health, prosperity, success, joy and peace. Through this perfect view our work as practitioners is one of delight, joy and enthusiasm.

As practitioners our main principle is to view our creation as perfect. We see the absolute truth of everything and everyone in our world. A practitioner looks beyond apparent, temporary illusions and thereby creates the eternal reality of all that exists in our life and world.

We as practitioners put our total attention to the fulfillment of this principle. It is the very essence of a responsible, successful and one-pointed practitioner. The results we experience by living according to this principle are magnificent and totally rewarding.

We practitioners tell our *friends* asking for prayer and healing treatment to write down or tell us of their positive healing request. Then we are aware of what our *friends* really choose to experience in their lives and they too know it as well. This is a very important aspect in our work and a wonderful tool to keep a positive attitude in consciousness. It teaches a positive discipline in thought and catalyzes our *friends* to be their own practitioner/healer.

This reminds me of a *friend* who asked me for prayer treatment in regard to his financial affairs. Our *friend* was telling me of all the problems and difficulties he was going through and that he did not see a way out of all this confusion. I talked to him and told him not to tell me of the problems and the things he did not want to experience but

The Practitioner's Principle

to speak about what he would really visualize for himself. As soon as he did, he realized what limiting causes he had continuously placed into motion by telling everyone of his problems instead of the solutions. He really had an illumination and everything regarding his financial affairs worked out beautifully, perfectly.

We always work with this eternal principle which uses the Law of cause and effect. Wherever we put our attention there is our experience. This is the principle of life: the principle of a successful practitioner.

Just as there are as many ways of meditation as there are conscious beings in the universe, so there are as many definitions for PRINCIPLE, the foundation governing essence of the cosmos. Each definition is correct. Each definition is complete and worthy of following. Dr Ingeborg Puchert points out that *we practice principle, the art of being ourselves, in letting go*, caring exclusively about ourselves. This remarkable definition truly depicts the ultimate understanding of principle—the art of being ourselves. For wherever we are or go, we are at all times reflecting back from our creation what we believe (know) about ourselves and our creation express in exactly the way we create them expressing toward ourselves and others. Dr Puchert captures this concept very well.

The Art of Being Ourselves

*W*e understand there is one universal principle. We accept the art of principle as the art of being that which we are. We live by this one principle. Living by this one principle means to us the way of how we express ourselves in the world in which we live.

Being ourselves means knowing the truth about ourselves and being true to ourselves. We know the truth about ourselves is that we are God. Whatever we think about ourselves is the true expression of the God presence in us for we are it. We are it, as we listen within we listen to our own inner self. We follow what we hear from within and in this way we are true to ourselves.

We practice principle, *the art of being ourselves,* in letting go. Letting go means that we care exclusively for ourselves. We mentally act in this way in the knowingness that whatever we see and define is exactly that what we experience in our life.

We enter a conference room and immediately we know that our presence is welcome by the people sitting there, for we welcome everybody of the assembly. We talk about the principle by which we practitioners live. We uplift ourselves in seeing (creating) it in the others, the reflection of what we think about ourselves. We accept the opportunity of this meeting and share the love we have for ourselves. This is one possibility of publicly demonstrating to ourselves who and what we are. We do it freely without any feeling of need.

We know of our selfsufficiency in all areas of our life. We have thoughts of abundance. We go within for the abundance of our living and experience it. This is the practitioner's principle.

We see the payment of our bills without looking outside for help or assistance in getting the necessary money. In this way we are true to ourselves. We treat for our own wholeness, perfection, health, abundance, right action and love. Whatever we recognize and affirm for ourselves we see reflected in the life of our beloveds. We do it for ourselves without talking about it or claiming any reward or recognition from their part.

We have everything, we are everything and bring forth from within ourselves everything we think or speak of to ourselves.

The indescribable principle always using the Law of cause and effect is how Dr Katarina Suter describes the practitioner's principle. So we then define the LAW as being the absolute in its operation, not subject to emotions, to the relative conditions of human physical rules (laws, albeit only rules that are changeable), to change. Dr Suter lays out this concept forcefully here.

Impersonal Principle

*W*e as a practitioner live by one principle alone; it is the principle of all existence which uses the Law of cause and effect.

We as practitioners think principle: it is the one and only principle in the universe; the principle which is unchangeable, impersonal, the principle which is without judgment for whatever information it receives, the principle which is eternally at our service, ready to manifest in our world for whatever we speak our word. The principle unfailingly fulfills every thought which we think. The principle and our onepointed and disciplined thought is the tool with which we create our body, our world, our universe!

We have a wonderful garden. One morning we recognize that the leaves of our freshly sprouted lettuce are eaten up by some animals. As a practitioner aware of the principle we are without one thought of blame or anger towards the animal, for we know that we are the creators of our world and that whatever happens in our world we bring into manifestation through the use of the principle. As a disciplined and responsible practitioner we use the principle in a beneficial way. We see the whole garden in the white light of love, we visualize each vegetable and each fruit fully grown and ripe. We use beneficial thoughts for the creation of the garden, for we know that the principle is without judgment and fulfills any cause we put into motion.

The Practitioner's Principle

Being aware of the principle opens up the unlimitedness within our own being. Through being disciplined and onepointed in the use of the principle we are the absolute masters of each experience in our life.

The principle is effective throughout what we call the *known universe* and in its influence beyond what any telescope from our bases in outer space can reveal of the ultimate nothingness of creation to the substantive expressions everywhere. Dr Sylvia Maria Enz issues this directive for our attention as the ultimatum given each of us from our childhood from parent and teacher alike.

Principle Fulfills Commitment

*O*ften when we are asked why we do certain things we make the statement: it is the principle. We say this for example whenever we remember a commitment we have made for something and now recall it and carry it through. We remember having heard this statement from our parents and teachers who, once an order is given stick by it because—that is the principle.

This of course hits the nail right on the head. The practitioner's principle in dealing with all life existence is through the Law of cause and effect.

Principle governs our universe. We can therefore say that principle is the commitment to every cause we put in motion.

With every thought we think, with every word we speak we put a cause in motion and unless we change the cause the effect has to manifest in our world.

It is important for the practitioner (that means every human being) to keep track of his thoughts and words. In a group of monks we discuss the influence of radio music while driving in the car. We all agreed that as practitioners of truth we are open to every subliminal cause we put in motion and are aware that we program our consciousness with all the limiting statements we hear through all songs. Unless we put a new cause in motion, put our thinking on a desirable level of experience, we always harvest the effects of our thoughts.

The responsibility of a practitioner toward principle is to stay in the awareness of the original purity and integrity. We as practitioners do this by blessing every place in our physical and mental experience. We see all and everybody we meet in the pure white light of love.

By doing this we put ourselves in harmony with the cause of our reality. We as practitioners are aware of the original principle of all existence and our responsibility is to keep our awareness onepointed on the truth.

We live the principle by living stably and consistently the cause of our reality. We live in the awareness of light, in the oneness of our reality From this point of view we live the cause; the effect and the cause are the same. Our cause is: I am the pure white light of love and everybody in my world is this pure white light of love.

Practitioners so live in the aura and awareness of principle that the principle is one with all that they do. Dr Ilse Wenk lives in this awareness. She points out principle is the practice, and the practice is the principle. At times this could be confusing, however who is there who could ever separate the principle from the practice. For with no practice the principle is not evident and with no principle what could a practitioner practice. All is ONE!

The Principle and the Practice

*O*ur principle is to practice spiritual purity and spiritual mind treatment. We practitioners think, speak and act in the purity of our awareness.

The practitioner's principle is to always stand up for the truth under all circumstances. I remember during World War II we Germans all had food vouchers. My father had offers to accept additional bread from people who worked in his office. He talked to me about it. He said to me: *Ilse, I know you understand, we eat only as much as we legally buy with our food vouchers.* I understood. We stand up for principle.

Our principle is to remain in our consciousness thinking pure thoughts every moment of the day.

Jesus asked those who came to him for help: *What wouldst thou of me?* He saw in the consciousness of those who came to him for help the reflection of his own pure soul. Jesus saw everyone having everything as he had everything, being everything, as he.

We have many *friends* who come to us with healing requests. The help we give is to guide each *friend* into his own understanding, to help themselves.

Our principle is to create our *friends* knowing the Law, the only Law that exists. It is the Law of cause and effect. Every thought ever thought is the cause for every effect that happens in the life of everyone. When we think a thought, at that same moment, we experience the effect of this thought. Therefore the practitioner's principle uses the universal Law.

The practitioner's principle is to share all in love. We are whole and perfect. *Friends* we see whole and perfect. We always give to those thoughts the power upon which we think. We think only positive thoughts and enjoy life.

Our principle is to always be responsible for every thought we think, every word we speak and our every action.

The Practitioner's Principle

So loving a consciousness has never found its way out of Luxembourg in all the centuries of its existence as that of Dr Robert Rettel, computer expert, now taking the concept of the computer sciences and applying them to the role of being a practitioner. He sees the practitioner's principle as GIGO, what Goes In Goes Out. He says that putting in pure thoughts and pure actions into our mental computer brings out its like. But also when we put Garbage In (only) Garbage (comes) Out! It is all a matter of our choice. The principle operating through the Law gives the user whatever the user chooses to GIGO in his experience.

The Practitioner's Rules

*A*s practitioners we are guided in our life by one rule: the Law of cause and effect. We have one guiding line in our universe: the Law.

By every thought that we think we bring a result in our world. By every thought that we allow in our mind we create our universe. Every thought is a new cause, and we create anew our universe.

We recognize the principle as universal; we recognize it as valid for everyone. We realize it as valid all the time.

We know the principle; we study it. We understand that with every thought we bring a result in our universe. We know that we are the creator of our entire world.

As practitioners we apply the principle consciously in our world. We use it beneficially for us and all the people in our universe. We apply it diligently: we think positive thoughts. With full attention we dwell with all our thoughts on beauty, joy, harmony, peace, abundance. We think high, very highly of ourselves and everyone in our world. We see with the eyes of perfection and purity. We recognize ourselves as whole and perfect, as pure. We recognize the same wholeness, perfection and purity in everybody.

As practitioners we apply the principle all the time. When we see in our world a condition which to us seems less than perfect, we immediately put a new cause in motion, we look for perfection and we declare the condition as perfect.

As practitioners we have the privilege of knowing the principle. We take total responsibility for our thoughts, words and actions.

I apply the principle consciously in my world. I start the day with a treatment for myself. I state: *I think pure and perfect thoughts. I speak words of perfection and purity. In all my affairs I am guided by the indwelling divinity, the infinite intelligence in me; I let God in me be God as me and through me. I declare my entire universe as good and very good. This day I see perfection in every situation.*

The Practitioner's Principle

◆

The planet Earth is filled with five and seven-tenths billion people at the moment of this printing. Because things move so quickly, quite likely there are six billion people on this globe as these words are being read. Smile! Ah change, what a lovely experience you are in the lives of the multitude—your creator!

The practitioner's principle is defined as the Law of cause and effect!

This is too simple a definition, albeit quite true.

Principle Versus Law

Just as the *law* of mathematics is not mathematics, and the *law* of physics is not physics, so the LAW of cause and effect is NOT the principle.

The two, principle and Law, are so intertwined, intermeshed, and used by the principle (the Law does not use the principle, the principle uses the Law) that here we find the dividing line.

The Law is just the Law. It is not the principle and the Law does not make anything happen. The Law is a system through which the principle is performed and expressed, but without the principle *putting the Law to work* the Law would remain dormant and ineffective.

From this point of view we see that the principle includes far more than just a mechanism for accomplishing its purposes. The principle is the allness, the principle is the expression and still the nonexpression of all, the principle exists and expresses and does so regardless the presence of the Law or its lack of being present. The Law has but one purpose and that is to establish causes. The Law is not the cause nor the effect it establishes. The Law is the expression of the principle's decision to carry out its purposes.

While the principle is not the thinker behind all thought, in truth there is no thinker behind anything, there is only isness. For if there were a thinker thinking positively and relatively, there could not be an infinite principle which stands regardless of anything. The absolute expression would be watered down and the relative or human standards would be the reality domain.

The reality domain is where all just is, indefinable, inseparable, ONE! As such no identity is present and no nonidentity is present. This is inconceivable for the relative thinker. Yet it is true. No values exist for nothing has value. All just is and cannot be otherwise.

Ah the dilemma of seeking to put labels on anything.

For now let's enjoy what our practitioners have shared with us and step by step walk into the awareness of something far greater than we have yet conceived in our finite thinking. ∞

Theme Seven

ONE DAY IN A PRACTITIONER'S WORLD

*T*here are only full moments in the daily life of a practitioner. Every second a practitioner monitors his thought and determines specifically what are the causes he places in motion relative to the experiences he chooses to have as effects.

A practitioner's day is twenty-four hours. It includes every single activity, every thought, every word and all these experiences of *others* in his world. For a practitioner creates himself and he creates every *other* in his world affecting his awareness of their action, word or presence.

Though this sounds like a tremendous task, it is a simple action.

The entire life of a practitioner depends solely upon how onepointed he is and how sincere he is

One Day in a Practitioner's World

in accomplishing the purpose he sets before himself. As he chooses to live a dedicated, disciplined, determined, diligent life, he will do all those things which bring it about. The world pretends that it is subject to things which it does not want to experience. A practitioner knows that whatever it experiences it alone has created in its world and therefore it experiences just that.

Dr Ellen Jermini emphasizes the idea that we are in charge of our lives not only during our waking moments, but also during our sleep. Insofar as this is a relevant point, she insists that we take charge of our dreams before they happen. It is necessary to establish the direction of our dreams and when the symbolic representation reveals itself, we knowingly choose to understand these symbols and direct the emphasis they impune in our thinking and acting.

Dreams Are Effects of Thoughts

I as a practitioner am in charge of my life day and night. I am always alert and awake, also as I sleep. I know I am GOD; I know I am the creator of every life experience; I know that every dream experience is as real as I allow it to be in my consciousness. Dreams are effects of thoughts and thoughts are causes I put in motion which bring the results I alone want to experience. So as a practitioner I take responsibility to keep track of my every moment thought; I am the master of my selfcreated world, of my dreams night and day; I am the master every twenty-four hours, each day totally, yes always.

I, as the practitioner need little sleep, my life is based on inner peace and harmony. I lay down for a couple of hours and continue with my thinking. To think means to meditate. So I prepare myself to go to sleep. Before I enter this special state of meditation, I say to myself: *I am always alert, I am always the master. Whatever may be my dream, I control it, I change it, I put a new cause in motion and I experience the effect I want.*

As I awake in the morning or from any dream also during the day, I remember my dreams, I know their symbolic meaning and I know where I am in consciousness.

I enter the day with joy and love for myself. I bless my world and love everyone in my wonder-world, the spectacular mirror of my own thought world. I see my world radiating in light and love and give totally to my world what I am. I am unconditional love, I am total givingness, I am the source of goodness, health and wealth, I am the abundance of the universe. I am all that exists.

One day in a practitioner's world is my work, to be the boss every single moment of the day. As I am the creator of my world, I live without judging my world, I live in an unemotionally quiet, harmonious world, being my untouchable beautiful self.

One Day in a Practitioner's World

A practitioner never experiences an *accident* in his life. People do not enter into his life nor does he enter into their aura of light and love—he at all times exists in his perfect state. Whenever he feels he has drifted from this state of awareness, he claims his natural state and turns his attention to his reality which he experiences since it IS his reality. Dr Stefan Strässle reveals how practitioners live in a constant state of renewal of their perfect awareness.

We Are the Creator

I as a practitioner start my day by immediately affirming to myself who and what I am. I am the responsible one of my life, of my world and of my experiences. I conceive of these facts in my mind and consciously recognize the role of the creator I accept to play.

I as a practitioner know the ultimate and creative power of my thoughts. For this reason I think my thought and visualize my world as an expression of absolute perfection. I say to myself that everyone with whom I deal today—be it at my job, in my family or with any person I meet—is an absolutely happy, joyous, harmonious, healthy, prosperous, selfloving, intelligent, peaceful and selfconfident being, living and expressing the divine from within. This is the blessing I give to myself as I start my day.

Conceiving of this attitude about my creation, which ultimately is what I think of myself, I radiate a pure light in my world. Everyone in my aura of love, light and happiness immediately merges with the light and becomes one as it. It is a beautiful, overwhelming feeling of oneness. It is a togetherness of the creator and the created, being one, for both have melted together in, as, with and through the light where there is no shadow, no individuality, no limitation but only the presence of the universal spirit.

This is where I as a practitioner come from while creating my day. I remain absolutely one-pointed. Should I create any situation in my world which I choose to change, I take charge and put another cause in motion, by visualizing the effect I choose to experience. It is all a matter of being in control of my thoughts and of onepointedly visualizing the perfect image.

Things always work out perfectly for me as the practitioner when I take charge of any circumstance ahead of the time. For example: I went to town to run some errands the other day. As it is, there are very few parking places in the shopping center where I shop and usually people have to wait for quite some time until finding a free parking place. I knew this and took charge of it even before I left home. I spoke my word and visualized the perfect parking place for me. When I arrived at the shopping center, I just turned around the corner and there was my parking place.

One Day in a Practitioner's World

Always I as a practitioner take charge by visualizing my world and experiences, things work out beautifully and perfectly. This is how a day in a practitioner's world expresses itself.

Methodically Dr Ingeborg Puchert describes a portion of the actual day of the life of a monk in the Absolute Monastery. For the twenty-four hour period each person is intuned to their inner being and all activities are directed to impress upon each monk his self-created world of purity and perfection. Always it is his own decision, his own choice, his own creation. Dr Puchert lists the time segments in minute fractions showing that discipline is high on the call in developing humility and nonpossessiveness.

Monk Practitioners

I am a practitioner in the Absolute Monastery in Campo, California and get up at 2:30 am. I start the activities in my world early. I have a short ablution and a drink of my choice. I recognize that I am the white light in my world. In this white light of love I touch everything and everybody in my world.

I as a practitioner live and share in the family of monks in a house. At 2:50 am I gather in the living room. I sit on the floor and form a circle. In the middle of the circle there is a white candle. The flame of the candle is for me the symbol of the eternal light, the light that I am from within. I meditate and listen to one of the *Golden Voyage* music tapes. From 3 to 3:10 am I listen to an inspirational talk by one of my group. I rise and share an OM. During the OM I recognize my universal oneness as all that exists in my world and my universe.

The next activity is the morning treatment of 30 minutes and ends at 3:55 am. I walk through the campus and speak loudly to myself for 15 minutes one sentence and continue with another sentence. From 4 to 4:45 am I listen to my inner self in introspection.

The time from 5 to 6:30 am I use for writing a philosophical essay on a theme. The daily theme I receive from the abbot. This is a very exciting work for me.

At 6:30 am I gather for breakfast. The breakfast is prepared by the one who is on duty for cooking that day. I drink milk or coffee and eat toasted bread with butter, peanut butter or jam. Cheese, eggs, honey and sugar are also served from time to time. This is the training of being possessionless in respect of the various ingredients.

The time for cleaning the kitchen, the Monastery, watering the garden and the grounds is till 7:30 am. I make another treatment, walking outside in the morning sun and at 8:05 am when I get the assignment of my daily work.

One Day in a Practitioner's World

All the time I cherish my God presence within. I express the divine from within. This means I take full charge of my mental attitude and love myself. I am judgmentless, have positive thoughts and speak positive words.

This outpictures the world of a practitioner at the Monastery.

In conducting our daily activities Dr Katarina Suter directs our attention to the concept that this training intunement with our true self is an opportunity to express our genius. Every experience of being a practitioner is the work of polishing the diamond of purity and truth indwelling. *This*, said Professor Suter, *is the reason that we live.*

My Life, a Blank Sheet of Paper

I am a practitioner of life and each day, every instant of my life is my field of practice. Each day is an opportunity to polish the diamond within me, which is my divinity. To reveal and express my true nature, God, is the reason why I live. With eagerness, dedication, diligence, determination, discipline and great onepointedness I look at every instant of my eternal life as a blank sheet of paper on which I now write the story of my life. I am absolutely free to compose it in any way I choose.

For instance: I am a monk in a monastery. I get up at 2:30 am and listen to a morning introduction talk from one of my fellow monks. I listen to a talk of positiveness. I start my day with constructive and wonderful thoughts. I light a candle and look at its flame for one minute. I train onepointedness in thought through this little exercise. I sing an OM, an Indian mantra, and think of a desire in my heart. This is a powerful way to put a cause into motion. Further I write a letter to myself. In this letter which is built up on one theme with an illustration, I express myself totally positive. This is a wonderful programing for a harmonious and peaceful day. I go for a treatment walk during which I speak my word for a circumstance in my life of which I choose to be the master. I sit in introspection and listen to my inner voice. I train intunement as my true self, God. I do my daily work and fulfill each assigned task with absolute love. I give my best to all I do. Each assignment is an opportunity to express my genius. At meal times I share positive ideas with my fellow monks. I create a world of love and harmony around me. In my sharing I confirm myself, for whatever I see in the others is my own reflection. At the end of the day I watch a movie or go for a walk. In both experiences I look at outer pictures of my creation and find an inner meaning behind them. Through my positive attitude about myself and my creation I experience each manifestation of my thought as meaningful.

I look at the day of a monk and realize that the day of each being on planet Earth is created in a similar way. The goal of life is to be aware of my Godself. The way through which I achieve my goal varies in details but is the same in the whole. Each day is here for me to fill with my creation of perfection. Each day is a blossom of my divine self.

Daily the practitioner opens his book of life and specifically writes on its pages the selfcreated adventures and experiences of his choice. The pages are empty awaiting to be filled with the loveliest story ever written says Dr Sylvia Maria Enz. This is our most important work the practitioner-philosopher insists and equates the adventure to a selfchosen journey.

Visualize the Day into Beingness

I start a new day. A new adventure is such a rewarding moment in a practitioner's world. Every new day is an empty page ready to be filled with the loveliest story ever written. What a joyful recognition that I as practitioner write every word of it; I determine how uplifting, how happy, how adventurous it is.

I as a practitioner know that my most important work is to see it done, to see every cause complete and fulfilled. The first thing in the morning is to take the time to sit down and in this quiet moment visualize the day into beingness.

The beginning of a new day is like the beginning of a trip, of a journey. Before I go on trip I bless it. I take the time to surround the car with the pure white light of love. I visualize the road and every car and every person and every being on it in my pure white light of love. I mentally determine that the road that lies before me is a joyful and peaceful road. Always I see myself arrived at the determined goal of the trip. I know that I am there. In my illustration the goal is the end of the day when I am at home after a busy day looking at it with satisfaction.

My day and how I create it is my spiritual path. I create the journey to the awareness of who and what I am on planet Earth. I create the trip through the adventures of this dimension of time and space—always knowing that I am there, that I am at the end of my awareness journey.

Keeping this in mind I meet every situation during my day, during my journey with the knowingness of right action because in my mind the journey is complete regardless of the many side trips into the time and space adventure.

So I as a practitioner go through my day knowing that everything I do is purposeful and perfect on my trip. I keep the awareness of who and what I am awake and in this harmony I experience every moment of my adventure as a blessing and an experience of great joy.

The daily activities of a practitioner are primarily ones in which he directs his thought, word and deed to the fulfillment of his choices. He loves to create harmonious things happening at all times. Dr Ilse Wenk reveals how good preparation allows her to effectively work with those in her world whom she creates as examples of her own convictions. Though she speaks volubly she develops an awareness of seeing her friend speaking glibly also. Her fluency is her creation of his fluency!

I Believe in Myself

*E*ach day in a practitioner's world is a very special day. I as a practitioner live my life aware. I believe in myself. I live according to my belief. I practice love, diligence, discipline, dedication, determination and onepointedness and humility.

I have my morning prayer when I get up. I bless my life with good thoughts, good words and good deeds. I have meditations and introspections during the whole day.

My main goal is to work together with friends. Friends I call those who are called patients in the medical world.

I am just about to prepare myself for the visit of a friend I have known for six months. He thinks he has problems to express himself in words. My preparation is a meditation in which I see myself whole and perfect and my friend whole and perfect and thinking and talking as beautifully as everyone in his world. I see him radiant, vital and loving. I see that he loves himself and therefore everyone in his own world. He arrives. His name is Peter. He is a young man who never talked much in his life. Now he has a profession where he sells cars and he wants to be as eloquent as possible. He tells me of his success in the past week and how he improved his ability to speak. Every day he reads loudly out of a book about positive thinking I have given him and he is now full of joy where he recognizes his success in his world.

We talk again as always about the Law of cause and effect. The practitioner's daily life is accompanied by thinking and talking about the Law of cause and effect. My friend Peter knows how important his thought is and he now thinks that he is the most eloquent man in the whole world. And he is!

It is so easy to slip away from our divine center either as a practitioner or as a normally active human being. Each time we do this we lose contact with our reality and therein suffer what we call accidents and unexpected or less than harmonious experiences. Dr Robert Rettel points out forcefully that a practitioner is so well grounded and prepared in the art of being a practitioner that should such conditions arise even slightly, the immediate response is working with another cause termed beneficial. He points out that even fleeting thoughts of working with household service people can end positively when the practitioner consistently and constantly maintains the proper mental attitude.

God In Us As Us Knows

I start my day in God and as God. I make conscious contact as God in me: I start in the morning with a meditation, a treatment. I think about my Godself, I treat for myself and my universe. I tune in to my divine center and communicate as God in me. I listen to the inner voice with a pure heart. I treat for joy, peace, harmony, goodness and divine right action. I know the inner God is the guide for all my activities.

All day long I deal with spiritual principles as cause and effect, love, meditation prayer, visualization.

I control my world by my constructive thoughts; I watch my thoughts and put beneficial causes in motion for me and my world. Each time I experience something that I call less than harmonious I put a new cause in motion.

I give out love to my entire world, to every person; I send out my love to every being, every plant, every object of my world. I love myself.

I do my work in the outer world; but as a practitioner I work from the inner: I do my work with the right attitude of mind and I use the Law. I have joy in my heart, I persevere in the face of seemingly difficult or impossible conditions. I know that I create every situation in my life, so I use the Law to create it well. I face my tests with courage and perseverance. I keep my thoughts always positive, on the spiritual reality that I am, regardless of the outer conditions.

During the day I take my time and meditate upon my real self, my divinity. I think about how I express my Godself.

I start the day with a treatment and a meditation. I see my work in the office on the computer as pure joy; I visualize harmony with all the colleagues at work; I visualize peace, harmony, friendly relationships with the users of the different departments that I meet. I send out love to all; I send out my special love to the person with whom I create *less than harmony*.

As I program and test my computer in the office, or as I work at home, I observe my environment. When I detect an event that is seemingly unbeneficial for me I put a new cause in motion.

I order fuel oil for the central heating; I am told that shortly after 5 pm it will be delivered. I wait and wait; as I become anxious, I put a new cause in motion. I release all my preoccupations about the fuel, I become quiet. I bless the carrier of the fuel and I go on to another activity with peace in mind. The *miracle* takes place. Shortly thereafter the carrier arrives and all is in divine right harmony.

◆

There are many who desire to be practitioners but few are persistent sufficiently to achieve this effective goal.

Truly everyone is a practitioner. Everyone daily practices the art of being a practitioner. But in this practice, what KIND of practitioner are we! Are we practitioners of fulfilling the selffulfilling prophecy of race consciousness, or are we fulfilling the individual God-choice arising from the spiritual core of our very being. This is a choice each makes. For the mass of humanity it is easier to *go with the flow* and not fight the current of public opinion, public sentiment and public judgment. Mob rule rules!

A practitioner of spiritual reality chooses what its values are and then sets all into motion which demonstrates the fulfillment of these virtues.

Essentially, it is difficult to know what the spiritual values and virtues are, but not to a one-pointed dedicated practitioner. A practitioner through introspection listens within himself to the universal God presence and is ever guided aright. There can never be a mistake.

All the guidance of a practitioner may not result in acceptability in the world. For it means going against the tide and fortune of the majority. It means standing up for principle. It means realizing that the Law of cause and effect is operative regardless whether we gain benefit or loss. Truly, all is our attitude. The practitioner's attitude is enhanced by daily listening in introspection to the divine within and following it flawlessly.

This takes onepointedness and discipline and humility. A practitioner is willing to give what it takes to achieve this. ∞

Theme Eight

THE VALUE OF POSITIVENESS

To enjoy the value of positiveness one might consider just what the word positive means. Every thought, word and action is positive. Every thought, word and action! Normally we think a positive thought, word, or action is one which is beneficial and harmonious in its application. FALSE!

When a negative action is completed, it is a positively negative action. When a fighter hits another in the boxing ring, it is a positive punch. Everything is positive. Since everything is positive, wherein does negative fit? Negative is anything we experience which is seemingly contrary to our choice. However, a cause, and it must have been our cause because the experience takes place in our life, was executed to bring that result.

The Value of Positiveness

All is issued forth out of a cause. All causes are positive. It is our privilege to determine which positive causes we desire to experience. None has the value of negative or positive (i.e.: good or bad) as a quality to it. Each only has the expression of having been utilized by us or not so utilized.

The value of positiveness lies in our choice. We either do or do not. The judgment begins and ends in this simple statement.

Dr Ellen Jermini has experienced the value of positiveness in many ways in her life, not the least of which has been in the effectively working with many parents whose children were doing poorly in their school lessons. She has had a large number of opportunities to work with parents and children in programing themselves, the children, and all in the child's world to recognize the child is a genius—and you had better believe it!—and so it was.

Mommie, Call Me a GENIUS, Please!

*W*e practitioners know the importance, the great value, of being positive in our thinking, speaking and acting. Each word we speak, each action we do, we diligently choose based on our onedirected positive thoughts. Positive thoughts we determine as thoughts which bring positive, beneficial results in our life, thoughts, we as causes put into motion by using the universal LAW, the Law of cause and effect.

So we say, we practitioners live a positive, beautiful, harmonious, successful life based on positive thinking. How do we understand this in our everyday life: For example we hear a mother complain about her son being an unsuccessful student at school. She is worried about his future life and about the child's promotion to the next grade.

We practitioners have the joy to talk to the mother and explain to her the value of positiveness in thinking. We stand firm on our own belief knowing who and what we are and with our definite positive attitude for a successful life, we confirm to the mother the indwelling genius in each child, in each being on this planet Earth. We are gentle and loving in our talk to the anxious mother, confirming the truth about our own life, knowing the reality of life. We exude brilliance and excellence through selfrespect and selflove, we radiate an inner peace and harmony, we shine forth our God presence.

We share with the mother our miracle sentence which works for children and adults, for everyone and repeat with her speaking out loud: I know that I know that I know, God in me is the answer.

After a couple of months we meet the mother again. She is so happy, she is so thankful, she joyfully tells us about her son's promotion and the great change in her and her son's life. She says: *It works, it is truly wonderful, yes it is a miracle. I am, we are now positive, we practice positive thinking.*

We know that miracles are effects, effects from thoughts, our thoughts—causes—we put into motion with the power of our own positive, one-pointed, disciplined thinking. We are the creators of our world, we determine what we want out of life, we are the masters of any experience in life, we are positive beings.

A practitioner gets just as excited as the friend. The practitioner knows the reality domain in which all just is and no judgments befall. The friend may be aware of the causes which brought limitation into his life or he may not. To the practitioner this is totally unimportant. The practitioner only works with CAUSES. The practitioner knows no old or new causes—only causes. Dr Stefan Strässle demonstrates mastership in positive causes and recounts their value here.

Positive, the Substance of Dreams

To be positive is the greatest value in the life of a practitioner. Being positive is what makes dreams come true, what makes mountains move and crumble down in the ocean, what makes us walk on water as though it would be solid rock, what makes us walk on fire as though we were walking over cool wet moss; being positive is *healing the less than perfect*, is turning poverty into wealth, stupidity into intelligence, war into peace, failure into success, disharmony into perfect harmony, and on and on.

All of these powerfully positive and beneficial virtues are achieved through specific, positive thoughts and the positive selfimage of us practitioners.

We practitioners positively visualize the picture we choose to experience, whatever it may be, remain onepointed on that very image, then inwardly conceive of the absolute knowingness of the picture's fulfillment, release it and think no longer about it. We put our attention on other things. These steps are the perfect preparation, the perfect overall cause we place into motion to experience *the* effect we choose. Now the channel is prepared for the new circumstance/condition/experience to enter our lives and affairs and be permanently in our world.

For us practitioners to be positive—as for everyone else in this entire universe—is the key word to a happy, healthy, prosperous, peaceful and harmonious life. The more we apply positive attitudes, the more positive experiences we have and out of that, the positiveness compounds itself and pretty soon our entire consciousness it totally expressing positiveness in all we think, speak or do. Then, we look at our world with totally new eyes—the eyes of a positive being, a master practitioner.

This reminds me of a friend who came into my life a couple of years ago. He had a very low selfimage and he did not think of himself as being intelligent, interesting, loveable or handsome or any other of the positive virtues normally admired in a person. So I worked with him over a period of time and I told him that he is a beautiful, intelligent, interesting, loveable and a handsome person. On and on I spoke absolutely positive regardless of the apparent limitations. After a short time he made an absolute turn-around in his selfimage. He started to talk positively about himself, his life, his job and his parents. His aura about himself changed completely. Now everybody liked being with him while before no one wanted to get too close to him. Of course his total life changed in all areas and today he is as selfconfident, happy, intelligent, interesting and as handsome as ever before.

This is what being positive accomplishes in our lives when we onepointedly stick to being positive under all circumstances.

Dr Ingeborg Puchert utilizes a rather earthy illustration to point out the value of positiveness. In recognizing value as money or barter items, she notes that sometimes seemingly greater *value* is paid for something because it is according to the exchange ratio rather than the actual value ratio. This is a most unique appraisal of the VALUE OF POSITIVENESS and reflects a humanistic approach to the utilization of words so common in our world today. Yet in citing this Dr Puchert reaffirms to each of us the value is relative and variable. It behooves us well to consider how much we are objectively or subjectively paying for anything before we actually extend such a price

Be True to Terminology

*W*e read the words *the Value of Positiveness* and consider what is the meaning of value and positiveness. We make sure what is meant with these two words. The word *value* means the worth we give to something. We evaluate something according to or for the price we pay for getting or buying a relative, material object.

With the word price we refer to money or the value of the good we offer in exchange for the good or service we desire. We have eggs and offer them in exchange for a breakfast for three persons. The coffee shop owner accepts the eggs we give for the price quoted for breakfast. We agree although the market value of the 12 eggs is higher than the breakfast. In this case prevails the desire for breakfast regardless of the value of the eggs. We work positively in consciousness in the knowingness that we have the perfect manifestation of the material object.

Looking at this circumstance from the point of positiveness, we practitioners are the creator of our world and create for us everything. We put the

The Value of Positiveness

cause in motion for breakfast and lo and behold we are invited for a breakfast, a breakfast free of charge. In this case we accept the offer without giving any value of money to it, for we consider only the fact. Our acceptance is the price we pay.

We also know that whenever we estimate or consider the material value of something, we judge that good for the worth we think it has for us. We practice positiveness and this we understand means judgmentlessness. We look for the positiveness in everything and we find it and flow with it.

We are practitioners and have a positive attitude about ourselves, our actions and the circumstances we create in our world. We act out of the spiritual understanding we have of ourselves and our actions. We experience the universal abundance where all things are without determining their value.

Wise words flow out from the purity of the heart, so well exemplified in the writings here of minister-at-large in Switzerland and Australia Dr Katarina Suter. *Each experience we create is without any value in itself*, she whispers here, yet her words are as the most tremendous cyclone roaring through the heavens. Thus the concept of THE VALUE OF POSITIVENESS is succinctly revealed. We determine whatever value there is in our experiences and call them positive as we choose, since we are the sole creator of all that happens in our world.

Positive Experiences Can Be a Habit

*A*s a practitioner we know the Law of cause and effect and its use in our life. We know that whatever we think about manifests in our world. We know that our thought is the cause of each experience in our life. In this awareness we know we are the sole creator of our world. We have the freedom to experience anything we choose.

Our desire is to experience a happy, fulfilled, peaceful, harmonious, abundant, limitless, joyful, lovely, healthy and balanced life. These are all positive virtues. As a practitioner we concentrate our thoughts onepointedly and with great discipline on positiveness. We program our mind with all the wonderful thoughts we choose to experience. We spend all our time in thinking about positive experiences. We make it a habit; we create it as our natural way of thinking.

We look out of the window and it rains heavily. Instead of thinking: *Oh my, this heavy rain washes out of the soil all the seeds which we have just planted*, or *now we have to sit inside the house instead of having a nice walk in the sunshine*; we rather think: *how wonderful, this rain is just what we need to settle the newly sown seeds firmly into the soil,* and *a walk in the rain, feeling each drop of this pure water on our skin is such a special experience.*

Each experience we create is without any value in itself. We give it value. We give it the value of positiveness which results in constructive, fulfilling and meaningful experiences. We have a positive attitude about ourselves and see it reflected in our creation. We look for the positive in all things for this is where we choose to have our experience. The value of positiveness lies in the experience of a positive life.

As a positive being we are fulfilled within ourselves. We are complete and know of the eternal source within ourselves. As a positive being we give all we are without the expectation of anything in return.

We are the ones who make the choice on what we dwell with our thought. Wherever our thought is there is our experience.

At the moment . . . we put the cause in motion for an undesirable effect, we are, for whatever reason, harmonious with this thought, inveighs Dr Sylvia Maria Enz in her discussion on the value of positiveness here. It is not so much a matter of questioning why or for what reason the inharmonious thoughts were instituted, but what do we want to do about it now. So to bring about a new experience, a new set of values must be expressed in positiveness. This requires of us a *positive awareness.*

For Whatever Reason, Now Think Positive

*W*e as practitioners know that positiveness is the harmonious expression of what we know as our real self. Every positive thought supports us in expressing our real self, our divine nature. To find out what is positive for ourselves is easy. Every experience that is harmonious with our thinking, every experience which lets our body feel good and harmonious, every feeling we like to experience again and again—is a positive awareness.

We as practitioners may ask why we ever experience anything which is less than our desire for ourselves and the answer of course is, that **at the moment when we put the cause in motion for an undesirable effect, we are for whatever reason, harmonious with this thought**. Once realizing that the expression of lack is not our true desire we put a new cause in motion to experience the positive, the beneficial aspect of our adventure.

Positiveness is constructive, uplifting and rewarding. Positiveness brings us in accord with the abundance idea of our reality. We all know the example of the glass of water which can be half-full or half-empty and we know that however we look at it, it is an experience of abundance or one of lack for us. We all know that the positive rewarding way of looking at it is to see it half-full. Looking at the glass as half-full we consider a positive attitude. Positiveness is exactly this: to

The Value of Positiveness

look at every experience in our life and see it as good and beneficial.

With this attitude we train our consciousness to the acceptance of positiveness, to the acceptance of the fulfillment and the completeness of our being. Doing this we manifest positiveness in all areas of our life.

Our daily work is to affirm our reality everyday, every moment of our existence. We are practitioners of truth throughout our whole experience on planet Earth. We as practitioners are alert and alive to happiness, joy, peace, harmony and love only. This is easy because as we listen within we know all these positive virtues as expressions of our true self. We recognize them as valid because as we express ourselves totally in it we feel ourselves in absolute harmony with our world, with everything and everybody in it.

Positiveness is the attitude that transcends appearances and we see everything in the light of truth. All is good, all is God.

Every thought is a cause! This is the conviction of Dr Ilse Wenk who has spent decades translating into many languages and out of many languages. Often in her translation she has had cause to ruminate over the true intent of writers and lecturers. So long as she sincerely chose to think in the author's frame of reference she produced effective information. Whenever she presumed for the author, she failed to effectively translate for them. So it is up to the practitioner to not presume what the world wants, what others (our creation) want, or what we are expected to want—as a practitioner utilizing the value of positiveness we know: *life is positive—just think positively and you experience it.* Dr Wenk conclusively relates the effectiveness of positiveness!

Every Thought Is a Cause!

*A*s practitioners we think only positive thoughts, speak only positive words and do only positive deeds. All is positive. Whatever we experience is positive.

The value of positiveness is limitless. We all live according to the Law of cause and effect. Every thought we think brings about positive effects *as every thought is a cause.* So whenever I think a positive thought the positiveness returns to me in the same moment. Every thought we think powerfully and positively brings about the strong powerful effect we have put into motion.

Our positive thoughts are limitless. We think, speak and act in diligence, determination, dedication and discipline, humility and onepointedness; and when we think these beautiful thoughts we experience happiness, peace, love, understanding and joy.

The Value of Positiveness

Everything is positive. The value of positiveness is limitless. We meet friends who say: *We do not always feel positive in life.* We tell them: *Life is positive just think positively and you experience it.*

We all live according to the wonderful Law of cause—every thought is a cause—and effect. The effect is the absolutely equal result of the cause. When we think a powerful thought, joyful and gentle at the same moment, the result of what we experience will be joyful and gentle. When we think a thought and we are quite sure that we want this, then we experience something according to our belief, according to our thought.

Practitioners are always winners. We train our mind and our treatment is positive thought. Practitioners know the value of positiveness as positive thought brings about positiveness. Therefore, whenever we talk to our friends who come to us for guidance we point out the fact that every thought is a positive thing and that: *What I think I receive as an experience. Only I am responsible for my thoughts.*

The value of positiveness bases on the positive thought, positive word and the positive deed. *I am a positive thinker.*

So often attitudes shine forth as the glowing armor around which we surround ourselves and in which we stand steadfast. Dr Robert Rettel shows in a bevy of words how *we practice all day long.* He issues the conviction that as we look from the highest viewpoint we see the innate purity in all. His is a glowing universe filled with harmony, peace, love and abundance. The same universe Professor Rettel enjoys he contemplates for all of his creation.

Attitudes, Knights in Shining Armor

*W*e keep our thoughts always positive. We are joyous, harmonious, peaceful and loving practitioners. All day long we practice positiveness: we dwell with all our thoughts on the beauty of life, on abundance. We put all our attention on perfection and wholeness. We put our onepointed concentration on purity. With all our heart we give out love; we send out thoughts of peace. We know who and what we are; we know our divine reality and we keep this in the foreground of our mind. We see our entire universe from the highest viewpoint: *We see the innate purity in all.*

Our attitude towards life is always positive: we expect the very best out of life. We get back from life that what we give out, that which we are. We get back all the positiveness that we spread out in our universe: we experience beauty, harmony, joy, abundance, peace. We plant seeds of purity and we harvest purity. We dwell on wholeness and perfection, and our entire universe is whole and perfect. We think divine, pure thoughts, in accord with our inner divinity and we know divine situations, we experience all the beauty, all the joy, all the harmony, all the good-

The Value of Positiveness

ness, all the abundance and all the peace of the entire universe.

We recognize the importance of our thoughts; we recognize that with every thought we create the experiences in our life. We are beauty, joy, peace, harmony, purity, perfection and wholeness. We are all good things. And with all our heart we dwell on our innate purity and we experience the reality of our real nature right now: purity, perfection and wholeness.

I treat for harmonious, divine relationships in my universe. I see the innate perfection in my creation; I send out thoughts of love to every person in my world. I flood with divine love every place where I am. I create harmony, peace within myself. I calm all my thoughts; I dwell in peace with all my heart. I experience peace, harmonious relationships with absolutely everybody. My relationships are friendly; I experience absolute harmony with the colleagues at work.

◆

To effectively achieve the highest adventure of life requires that we maintain the purest and greatest value of positiveness in our thinking, in our speaking and in our living.

To achieve this requires diligence and discipline to the utilization of this perfect value, this perfect positiveness.

It can easily be done. The easy part is that it can be done. The hard part is the humility required when we look away from past experiences which are *real* and *solid as rock*. As we look at the relative universe it is as quicksand that mires us deeper and deeper into illusion. We get to believe the illusion and in this belief credit it as truth and we are lost.

To elevate our attitudes from yesterday to today means that we put an entirely new set of conditions in motion for ourselves. This is truly easy. And sincerely, there is no hard part. The humility is to say ok we will try it. The discipline is to try it when the learning and expressing of it does not seem to bring immediate results. And the joy and confidence of staying with it all results in miracles. Smile. ∞

Theme Nine

THE PRACTITIONER A FRIEND TO ALL

What does it mean to be a friend of all? It is far from what it might be considered that it would mean.

The practitioner is nonjudgmental, unconditional, absolutely loving, caring with empathy, staid to the principle unfaltering—living according to the words of Jesus the Christ wherein he asks those who come to him: *What wouldst thou of me?* He never judged or advised anyone, he only showed the highest and finest way in which they could achieve the choice—desires—of their heart and soul.

A practitioner is a friend to all because he has no bias, bigotry, no sense of differentness relative to anyone else in the universe. It would not matter

The Practitioner a Friend to All

the color, religion, design of face or body, regardless how uniquely different a being may be—the practitioner is totally one as all.

Practitioners themselves working in this area are somewhat jaded in their ability to express an opinion. The reason: They have no opinion! It does not matter to a professional practitioner how right or wrong, good or bad, tall or short, mean or ugly a friend may be—to the practitioner the only question asked is: *What wouldst thou of thyself? You set the new course in motion for yourself and I will show you the program through which you can achieve whatever is the desire of your heart.*

Could anything be any less judgmental, less conditional, more universally loving! Smile!!!

Noteworthily Dr Ellen Jermini, abbess of the Absolute Monastery, looks through her own eyes at the idea of *friend* and comprehends this creation from her own vision of herself and her world. Truly, as the abbess recounts, *There is no secret to being a friend of all.*

I Am My Own Best Friend

As I read: *The Practitioner A Friend To All*, the question immediately comes up, what secret remedy do I as a practitioner use to say I am a friend of all, yes to say, the world is mine, to say my world is magnificent.

I as a practitioner know the treatment, the special way of living a successful, harmonious, peaceful life; I know the secret of true, everlasting friendship; I know that friendship—any friendship—starts and ends with myself alone. The secret, however, lies hidden deep in my inner, in the precious place of inner knowingness, the wisdom of being; I know who and what I am! However, I have the choice to enter this wonder place to dig in it, (introspection) to search the great treasure, (to listen within) to find the gem of inestimable value. Yes, here indeed I find my friend, my best and true friend, I find myself one as all, united in the world of minerals, plants and animals. I find myself, a divine being; I recognize myself a friend of all.

For example I am on trip and I spend a night on a camping ground. Soon I recognize people coming closer to me and talking to me. I hear our neighbors asking me questions about life, I hear them posing the question why I appear so happy, why I exude such a charisma of joy. I explain to them my way of living, I explain to them my positive attitude of life, I tell them that I alone am the master and creator of my own life and that I love what I do, that I love myself, that I am my own dear friend.

In the revelation and recognition of myself THE FRIEND, and sharing it with the world as myself the great power, myself God, I confirm myself the friend of all; I live a special relationship, I live harmoniously with myself. This reflects back to me, toward my world as a mirror of absolute self-respect, unconditional love, it reflects my own attitude in life.

To practice unconditional love as a human-divine being, I practice living the truth about myself, I live my life based on my God presence, I live in my introspective self, I live in my reality domain. I a practitioner know my relationship as God, myself, I am one as God, I am all as God, I am God, I am friend of all.

Using the editorial *we* Dr Stefan Strässle reviews the concept of a practitioner being a friend of all and divines perfect humility with everyman! Those who were most significant and friendly with all mankind were *accomplished* friends to themselves first, Dr Strässle points out, not only to man but animals and plants and all animate and inanimate life.

Friend to Themselves First

*T*he practitioner is a friend to himself first. That means as practitioners we like our own company, we like to be in our own presence and feel fulfilled from within our very being. We love ourselves.

Every practitioner is closest to his own self and finds the harmony, the peace and the happiness within himself. A successful practitioner's wellbeing is independent of how he creates other people's presence, however a practitioner enjoys sharing with friends.

Friend generally means that there is a special feeling of oneness, love and togetherness. It is a harmony, a peace, an understanding being expressed between two individuals. It is an inner knowingness/charisma of the perfect love, an unconditional and nonjudgmental giving from self to self, melting together as one. This is what friend means. The accomplished practitioner has found all of these virtues within himself and demonstrates, lives, expresses, and shares his *being a friend* with his world.

Therefore we can say: THE PRACTITIONER A FRIEND TO ALL. A practitioner is a friend to everyone and all: person, animal, mineral and vegetable. As practitioners we are one as all.

Thinking of these ideas we practitioners are reminded of the many saints like *St. Francis of Assisi* and other practitioners who demonstrated perfect oneness with animals, or *Jesus the Christ* who expressed perfect love with the people he lived with. Both were *accomplished friends to themselves first* and lived that friendship with all.

This is what we as practitioners do: we live who and what we are. We always do that since all our world is a reflection of ourselves. Therefore we can say that we are always a friend to all exactly in the way as we are a friend to ourselves. We practitioners love ourselves totally and share that love with everyone and everything in our life.

The Practitioner a Friend to All

The practitioner, a friend of all, brings to the mind of Dr Ingeborg Puchert, a friend being a person of whom we are fond and in whom we find the virtues of honesty, loveliness, knowledge, wisdom and right action. Naturally this is but a reflection of what we are within ourselves, seen in the friend. She states categorically, a practitioner is a friend upon whom we may call at any time. We all stand with the practitioner, standing firm and express the divine from within.

A Person of Whom We Are Fond

*W*e read the words A FRIEND TO ALL and recognize the broad area of what is meant. With the little word *all* we mean **all**, the allness without referring to a specific item, action or the consciousness as, in and through it.

We consider a friend a person of whom we are fond. In that friend we see the virtues of honesty, loveliness, knowledge, wisdom and right action. In the practitioner, a friend of all, we recognize the virtue of being true to himself. This is one of the priorities the practitioner applies in his life and hence he is a friend to all and of all. We recognize the inner light of a pure consciousness, the sparkles of a diamond within.

We say that person is a friend, a friend of all. The primary task of a practitioner is to see his own allness. This is the basis for a practitioner in being a friend of all. The practitioner sees himself in everybody in his world. Along with the commitment the practitioner makes to himself in seeing in others himself he takes responsibility for it. He freely and joyfully exercises this responsibility without asking for anything in return.

A friend of all is all within himself. He is the source of all and has all the very moment he thinks of something.

In the practitioner we recognize the one friend upon whom we can call at any time. In the practitioner we see the living example of what he professes as truth about himself. The friend knows the truth about himself and sees the same truth shining forth in everyone he meets. To a friend who sees the good, the benefit in whatever situation, all clouds and blocks fade away and a clear canvas appears.

We know there is only one truth and that truth is that we are all that there is. That all, the allness we name God and freely proclaim that we are God.

The practitioner stands firm and expresses the divine from within. The practitioner indeed is a very special friend. He expresses his virtues in a silent friendship. He knows the real value for himself of the silent friendship. The good this kind of friend sends out in consciousness unfailingly returns to him. He exercises the Law of cause and effect in the simple affirmations he makes about himself.

The Practitioner a Friend to All

A heart as big as all outdoors has Dr Katarina Suter, yet she chooses to equate friendship in her example here as an inanimate object—a tree! Truly, we are friend of all. This allness includes everything. The wisdom of few are grand enough to encompass the inanimate things of their life from the first person, present tense, positive point of view. Dr Suter's tree does this!

A big Old Oak Tree, My Friend

*W*hat is a friend. We call a friend someone we feel harmonious with, someone we love, someone we honor and respect, someone with whom we share our thoughts.

We as practitioners know that all our creation is one. We know that each of our creation comes from the same source—our thought. This is why we say all is one. We are a thought and the world around us is an offspring of our thought. Our physical appearance is a manifested thought coming from the same source as all other creation—the oneness of all.

It sounds wonderful as we say we are a friend of all; however it is a natural inference or effect of our statement that we are one as all and all is one as us. Another reason why we are a friend of all is that we see our inner friend (our divinity) reflected in our creation. We see the oneness of our own being reflected in each creation, small or big, animal, mineral or vegetable. We see in all what we are—a divine thought.

A friend may be anything. As an example: We call a big old oak tree our friend. Why do we call it our friend when it is without a mouth with which it communicates, legs to go on a walk with us and eyes to tell us *I understand you!* We call the oak tree our friend because we talk in the language of oneness and have through it a perfect communication. We look at the strong stem of the tree and it talks to us of stability, steadfastness and standing up for who we are. We look at the limbs reaching out in all directions, gently moving in the wind. They talk to us about flexibility, unlimitedness and expansion. We look at the green lush foliage of the live oak tree and it talks to us about growth, positiveness, happiness and abundant creation.

We are in perfect communication with the tree through our recognition of the oneness as the tree. The tree is merely a sounding board for all we know within ourselves. Whatever friend we find in our creation is the friend we are within ourselves. We as practitioners see the friend in all for we are in tune with our inner friend—the divine.

To be a friend means to have a relationship with all of our creation, writes Dr Sylvia Maria Enz as she describes the practitioner, a friend to all. She illustrates how our attitude builds harmony in our world or how insecurity brings all of the limitations it is heir to. Once we are friends with ourselves, once we are at peace within ourselves, then all is in perfect working order. Truly, our world is a reflection of what we are within.

We Live in Oneness as All Existence

We as practitioners of spiritual truth live the awareness that we are a friend of all in all areas of our life, be it people, animals or nature in general. *To be a friend means to have a relationship with all of our creation.* In the definition of a practitioner it means that we live in oneness as all existence.

The entire universe is a reflection of our awareness about ourselves and so consequently is also the universe of plants and animals. They respond to us with exactly the expectation we have of them. They always reflect the thought we have about them.

We all know this is true for plants. We know that they respond to our loving attention with more growth with more flowers. We know this true for animals. We know that house pets, especially dogs, reflect exactly our thinking. We have a dog named Prince. When I first meet him he barks angrily at people coming close or into the house. We are astonished about his protective behavior—but quickly realize that his behavior has its origin in our own consciousness in our own over protective attitude toward ourselves and the Monastery.

We change our protective attitude and surround the house and the property and everybody who enters our world with the white light of love. The miracle takes place: Now with friendly curiosity every visitor is inspected and accepted by Prince—by us.

We as practitioners live in a world which naturally is in harmony with our true self as it is our reflection. Every being in our world reflects the balance and the peace that we are. Our relationship to nature is one of absolute oneness. We recognize this oneness in everything in our self-created world—and in this recognition we truly are the friend of all. We are one as all. We are all and we are in love with our creation. We live in harmonious oneness with people, animals, plants—all are friends—our creation!

The way to understanding our creation is to understand and love ourselves first, states Dr Ilse Wenk, as she states: *We practitioners meditate and pray all day long.* She insists: *We practitioners first reveal the divinity in ourself then we show the way to our creation.* These words are a model of the ideal of friendship.

We Love Ourselves

*W*e practitioners are our own best friends. We are a friend of all.

The Practitioner a Friend to All

We practitioners meditate and pray all day long. So we are always ready and alert to think good thoughts, speak good words and do good deeds. We like ourselves thus we like and love all our creation.

Wherever we go we are at home. We call our body the temple, the temple of the living God. We talk with all. All talk with us. We are friends of all.

We are only and totally concerned with our awareness. We are always smiling. We take total responsibility for our thoughts, words and actions. In this integrity and sincerity we can effectively treat. Therefore we are a friend of all.

We practitioners first reveal the divinity in ourselves then we show the way to our creation. It is a joy for us practitioners to work together with our friends. We love our friends. We love all. And this is because we love ourselves. Only when we love ourselves can we love our fellowmen, can we love all.

This is how we work with our friends, with all who come to us for guidance. We first let the friend tell us all about his wishes and desires and then we ask them: *What do you want for yourself. Do you desire any changes in your life?* The friends answer. They sometimes want changes in their life. Then we talk about the Law of cause and effect. We tell our friend who wants a change in his life all about the Law of cause and effect, and how easily a new cause can be put into motion. Every thought is a cause and the effect equals the cause/thought. They love us all because we just guide and offer the way to the solution. We all have to find our way alone.

We are open minded and open hearted. It is easy to communicate with us. We love ourselves. We love our life. We love all our friends. We love all. We practice determination, diligence, dedication and discipline. We are onepointed and humble. We are a friend of all.

As a practitioner, it is sometimes tempting to say that everyone has the right to follow their own freedom of choice—this is contrary to a master, a practitioner, a leader in the field of spiritual awareness. A practitioner is a master and is a friend of all because the practitioner has first created all who are his friend—he has created all. Because of this, as Dr Robert Rettel states, *We define a friend as someone on the same level as we, our creation.*

We See a Friend

*W*e see all in our world as friends; we see purity, perfection and wholeness in all.

Whoever we meet in our life we see in him a friend. Whatever the condition is we see a friend.

We define a friend, as someone on the same level as we, our creation. We see in everybody a joyous center of peace, harmony, love. We see in everybody their reality: their innate purity, perfection and wholeness. We know about our spiritual reality and we recognize in everybody this same reality. We see all as God. We recognize all whole and perfect.

We live a life of beauty, abundance and peace. We base our life on principle: we think pure thoughts: thoughts of joy, love and peace. We have the freedom of choice and we choose positive thoughts, pure thoughts. We recognize in all the same abilities and possibilities as in us; we recognize for all our creation the same perfection as for ourselves. We see everyone follow their own inner guide; we see everyone guided by their own inner teacher.

We see all as dear friends, all people in our world. We create in everyone as a reflection—of us—all that we are.

We base our life completely on principle; we create a world in accord with our beliefs, our entire universe is whole and perfect and everybody in our universe is whole and perfect. We show how the principle can be used for the highest good, but we create everyone to follow his own inner light. We discuss the use of the Law in our life.

I give freely, willingly of my knowledge about the Law to my family. I discuss the Law with my brother Nicolas. I show how I use it, how I speak my word for wholeness and perfection. I speak with him about an example from my work in the office, where I see everyone as a friend, where I see perfect cooperation of all and complete harmony. Nicolas accepts the principle as functioning well.

Practitioners are as temptable to being drawn in by the human attitude which says that everyone has freedom of choice to be and do anything they wish to do. If this were true, why would a practitioner work to bring harmony, right action, wholeness and peace into the experiences of anyone, why would a practitioner seek to pray or treat for anyone who in using their own techniques and freedom of choice and have created for themselves misery, hatred, unhappiness, poverty and limitation?

A practitioner is a selfcreated being who created every being who comes into their realm, their world. A practitioner does not give FREEDOM OF CHOICE to any of its creation. Neither did any philosophical/religious creator, for to do so would mean that only confusion reigns.

As a practitioner is a creator, as a practitioner is a professional, as the practitioner is a master in his realm, the master practitioner creates all in his world and all in his world reflect exactly what the master practitioner knows of himself.

If a master practitioner would allow freedom of choice to the friend in his activity, that friend could create experiences out of sync with the master.

All over in the world are an infinite numbers of beings who utilizing their freedom of choice echo lack and limitation and death in their experience. They do this because they have not chosen a way leading to eternal life, health, wholeness and perfection. This latter way is the way taught by philosophers through the ages and listened to and followed by all too few.

As master practitioners we create in our world our friends who reflect in every beneficial manner what we know to be true of ourselves. So if the reflection is anything less than we deem reasonable and right, we put a different cause in motion and benefit from it now and always. ∞

Theme Ten

THE PRACTITIONER A MEDICAL/SPIRITUAL HEALER

*E*very practitioner knows that before all else the practitioner heals his own consciousness and recognizes the reality of himself. In this state of awareness, the practitioner is whole and perfect. In this state of consciousness the practitioner can only see outwardly what he is within himself—whole and perfect. Thus, the friend with whom the practitioner works is also whole and perfect! This is the principle and the Law.

We do not change medical conditions nor do we change spiritual conditions.

All any practitioner does is to recognize what the pure medical conditions are and what the spiritual foundation is behind all of the outward expressions we have in life.

True, the practitioner is a medical/spiritual healer, but the healing is merely a recognition in the practitioner's consciousness of what is, was and always will be. Nothing new is added, nothing old is taken away, nothing is changed—only the truth is revealed.

This is the way and the only way a practitioner produces in his world.

We do not manipulate physical or spiritual rules—the Law. We put it into work and it works.

We do this to remember our reality, points out Dr Ellen Jermini, as she defines the program and purpose of a practitioner. In her illustration, the president of multinational corporations and exquisite practitioner, relates how she first purifies her own awareness of a friend before that friend can outwardly express and experience the wholeness which she is in the life of the practitioner or in the life of the practitioner's reflection, the friend! Smile.

Our Original Purity and Integrity

*W*e practitioners know that healing means to return to our original purity and integrity. Our original purity and integrity is our true, real beingness; it means to be our divine self, to be God in, as, through all that exists and be it nonjudgmentally, unconditionally.

We ask ourselves for what reason we create ourselves on this planet Earth, living in a human body—yet knowing ourselves to be a divine being, challenging our life with experiences such as healing apparent body diseases or illnesses. *We do this to remember our originality, our reality.*

I recall a friend who one day desperately called me asking for healing prayer. Her sister was in hospital and the doctors had given her just two weeks to live. She appeared terminally ill and only a miracle could save her life.

We practitioners however know that miracles are the effects of a disciplined use of the one great LAW, the Law of cause and effect. We practitioners know our responsibility in those illusionary moments where we are asked for healing and take charge. WE take charge one hundred percent of our own life, our world. We concentrate on the truth, knowing that we are the creators and the masters of our world and any experiences. Immediately we speak our word of power, we are one as the power, we are the indwelling power and visualize our world perfect.

So I acted in the case of my friend.

My friend—herself a dedicated and diligent practitioner—soon confirmed the expected miracle happening. The doctors were full of surprise but I understood/understand yes, I know that healing—any healing—is done in thought only, is done in my mind.

As we love and respect ourselves as that what we really are—God, the omniscience, omnipresence and omnipower—we fulfill our purpose in life: we live in the recognition of our divine self, we are our pure perfect selves! Through onepointedness in thought and selfrealization we live a happy, healthy life. We practitioners are a medical/spiritual healer by living our original purity and integrity. We know that we are whole and perfect, that we are one in spirit, mind and body; we are God.

Many would-be practitioners seek to manipulate the rules to gain an effect. We as practitioners put the Law in motion and let it function as it is designed to perform—staying absolutely out of its way so it can achieve its purpose once put into motion. Dr Stefan Strässle defines the field of healing in its general and specific areas. Physical healers work specifically while spiritual consultants are overall more general in their approach. Professor Strässle defines physical healers working with effects while practitioners of the spiritual wholeness program work totally with causes.

We See It Already Done!

*B*oth medical healers and spiritual healers are practitioners. Both strive for the same goal: to create and live in a harmoniously functioning world. That includes every person in a practitioner's life and experiences.

A medical healer works in the field of the wholeness of a being's physical vehicle. That means, a medical healer treats the specific healing needs in the body through medical treatment. A medical healer works with effects (i.e: symptoms) which means that his main concern is the return of an imperfect body to wholeness, without reflecting about the mental attitudes of the friend which caused the imperfection in the first place.

We as spiritual healers work in a much wider field. Our treatment for wholeness and perfection concerns all areas of life. Naturally it includes the physical body. However, it goes beyond that into the fields of prosperity, relationships, business life, social life and the big realm of spiritual self-awareness.

As spiritual healers/practitioners we work with causes. We concern ourselves with the overall wellbeing of a person which is independent of one area alone, as for example perfect physical health or prosperity. To outpicture perfect health or prosperity requires perfectly healthy attitudes in the consciousness of those with whom we work which of course means that we as healers/practitioners demonstrate perfect mental attitudes in ourselves.

To work with causes means that we put beneficial causes into motion. We direct our power and attention to the choice of our experience. To look upon the limiting effects means we empower them to be a reality in our lives. This is far from our choice.

To work with causes means that we work with the Law of cause and effect and onepointedly visualize (by our thoughts) the image we choose to experience and experience it.

This is how we as successful spiritual healers work. We always put our attention on what we want to experience, see it done and so it is. Our work is limitless and successful for we work with the Law of cause and effect, the spiritual Law that works under all circumstances, at all times and in every avenue of life.

The following is a comprehensive discussion on definitions and terms used in the medical and spiritual field for practitioners. Dr Ingeborg Puchert fully understands the programs of both fields and their relevance one to the other. Albeit, Dr Puchert lays full competence on the spiritual practitioner for effective work; this does not belittle the work of the medical profession, but merely places it into perspective.

Spiritual and Medical Healing

*H*ere we have a long title with two meanings referring to the activity of a practitioner. In the dictionary we find the following first explanation for the word *medical* with: *Pertaining to or employed in the science, study or practice of medicine or the art of healing disease.* With the word *spiritual* we refer to what is of spirit or the soul. We know the difference between spirit and the intellect. Now we understand the meaning of medical art and spiritual art of healing. To the one who practices the art of medical healing we give the title of medical doctor. We know that medical healing is based on improving the function of the various organs and components of the human body. We hear from these medical practitioners their medical success comes from some unknown power. We hear amazing effects are experienced with both medical and spiritual treatment. We also see that the effect of a medical treatment varies from patient to patient, from case to case.

We know of the reward we can take for the effect of our treatment for a friend in care of medical surgery. We see the astonishment doctors have in the case of disfunctions which at a second visit appear healed in a special or unusual way.

We call a spiritual healer a practitioner for he practices the art of spiritual healing without being concerned about the friend's physical condition or pain, when the practitioners get the request for treatment. We, the spiritual healers work on what the friend wants to experience without investigating or wanting to understand the pain or the disease. We practitioners live in the spiritual realm and these conditions and words are unknown

In our treatment we affirm the original state, the state of purity, wholeness, integrity and perfection about ourselves. In doing this mental work for ourselves we see its reflection in the condition of the friend. We bring the friend's awareness back to the original purity and integrity of his beingness.

In this connection we refer to the words of Jesus: It is done unto you according to YOUR belief.

We practitioners are the expression of the universal energy. We use the healing power from within, the reality of our beingness. We explain to the friend the eternal principle, the Law of cause and effect and how to use it in a beneficial way.

We, the spiritual practitioner, focus onepointedly our thought on the desire of the friend in the knowingness that we bring forth in the friend the desired condition.

Practitioners often speak words so effective that their few comments spell out the entire program and process of their work. Dr Katarina Suter has come to this in her last sentence stating: *As a spiritual healer we realize that we are without need to heal anything for we see all perfect—a reflection of our own being.* In so saying, Dr Suter has spelled out the entire work of either medical or spiritual healer—a true practitioner at work.

A Friend—a Reflection of Our Wholeness

*T*he basics of any healer is to recognize his own wholeness and to express it. Wholeness in body mind and spirit is our nature.

Our work as a healer is to recognize the wholeness in our fellowman as a reflection of our own wholeness.

We meet a friend and he starts telling us all about his backache and how it limits his movements and his work. We as a healer interrupt the friend gently in his explanation about the undesirable experience. We ask him what he chooses to experience. We tell him to take all the power and onepointedness he puts on the undesirable circumstance and put it on what he really chooses to experience. We tell the friend that we see him whole and perfect and that it is done. We tell him that as he speaks his word for his perfection it is done unto him according to his belief.

As a practitioner we play the role of catalyzer. We see wholeness in all of our creation and share our point of view with our creation so that they may see it for themselves. We are spiritual healers which means that all we use is the Law of cause and effect. We put the cause of wholeness into motion and experience it as an effect. We recognize that any medical treatment is only a temporary healing unless it is done as a symbolic act to accompany our word of wholeness. Spiritual healing includes everything. As a spiritual healer we see everything expressing its purity and perfection.

The Practitioner a Medical/Spiritual Healer

We may create some illusionary appearances of imperfection. In such a situation we affirm our wholeness through onepointed treatment. We know that our disciplined thought is what brings any expression into our world. We are the ones who make the choice what we like to experience in our life; it is so simple and so effective!

As a spiritual healer we realize that we are without the need to heal anything for we see all perfect—a reflection of our own being.

A plausible question is asked: Why do we need medical doctors? The answer is given by Dr Sylvia Maria Enz as she explains this is as all part of our growing awareness, our experience in finding ourselves. As in a game of chess, we know all the rules of the game as does our opponent. We play intelligently as does our opponent. We keep in mind ALL THE POSSIBILITIES as does our opponent—but in one little moment of forgetfulness we ignore a possibility and our opponent does not and he wins. In like manner the medical profession is likened to chess. However, the professional spiritual practitioner does not work with rules—only the Law—and the professional practitioner sets causes in motion so pure and true and onepointedly, the effect arises out of it regardless of the seemingly superior opponent.

It Is Done According to Our Belief

*H*ealing means to return to one's original purity and integrity.

We as practitioners know that there is nothing to heal but to get the awareness of who and what we are. The reason why we are here on planet Earth is to reveal this awareness of our reality. Our being on this dimension of time and space is the tool, the catalyzing experience, leading us to that inner reality, to that inner diamond which has always been there awaiting only our recognition.

Now if there is nothing to heal why should we ask the question about medical healing? We are the creator of our world. We create every experience in our life by our thought. Whatever and however we create the spiritual path is our decision alone. We create it in the way that responds to our individual psychology. We create challenges to prove to ourselves the understanding of our present awareness on the path. We create an illness or an experience of lack to demonstrate the power to speak our word, to put a new cause into motion and experience the positive, the wholeness aspect of our creation.

We know that all is done to us according to our belief. We create an illness and then speak our word for the wholeness of the body. With the awareness of this reality we may go and see our doctor and have this wholeness confirmed. We stand firm in this belief and it is done. We have a doubt—we go on taking the pills or the medicine which help the body to find a balance, but most important; we do our homework and strengthen our inner awareness to the total acceptance of the wholeness that we really are in body mind and spirit. We affirm our wholeness into beingness into existence until we are it in every area, in every little aspect of our beingness.

We as practitioners know of the illusion of appearances and live in the perfect balance, the perfect peace which is our true self. It is done!

Medical doctors describe their machinations as keeping the patient alive long enough so that the natural body functions can heal it. Dr Ilse Wenk wisely states: *Medical healing deals with the effect, spiritual healing deals with the cause.* Onepointed control of every thought we think, every thought thought by our friend, every thought allowed to be created in the cosmos by our acceptance of it as an important issue in our lives, a practitioner is always responsible.

Thought Is a Subtle Thing

*I*t is true we practitioners heal ourselves. All we do is show the friend how to heal himself. Hippocrates said: *Physician heal thyself.*

Medical healing deals with the effect, spiritual healing deals with the cause. That means when we attempt to heal medically then we treat the effect, the illness of the body. This is without any change. The only change that can be brought about is by treating in the spiritual way,

Every illness is caused by a thought. The thought is always the cause of any experience we have in our life. If we have an illness we have thought of it. The thought is a subtle thing. The thought is the cause of every experience we have. We practitioners work on our conscious thoughts. The practitioners are absolutely aware that healing is an individual matter. Therefore the thought alone is the healing factor.

We are in charge of all thoughts which we think. We practitioners think all our thoughts absolutely consciously. We practitioners return to our purity and integrity of our consciousness. We live the words the philosopher Zoroaster spoke: *To the pure all is pure.* And in the purity of our hearts we practitioners are healed. All are practitioners. So it is that we can direct all thoughts we think consciously.

It is true that we also think thoughts in our subconscious mind. Therefore it is unbeneficial when we think our thoughts subconsciously. A thought which comes into our mind subconsciously is probably much more powerful than a conscious thought. *The subconscious thought is without our control.* And to heal ourselves we have crystal clear thoughts of love and joy, happiness and peace and all the beautiful thoughts we can imagine. We practitioners explain to the friends how a new cause brings about healing. How a new cause is put into motion. This is what we do with the demonstration of the Law of cause (thought) and effect. *Man heal thyself.*

Remarkably well Dr Robert Rettel describes the art and action of a spiritual practitioner. A practitioner puts the Law in motion for himself and his world. That is the sum and substance of it. We recognize one healer: *Me!* This is the only creator in our world and what we create, what we see outwardly as the reflection of ourselves, is our world, our vision. *I realize that it is done according to my innermost belief.* Dr Rettel is quite clear in this conception.

Health Is the Result of the Correct Use of the LAW

As practitioner we put the Law in motion for us and our world. We use it consciously for our highest good; health is the result of our correct use of the Law.

We recognize our innate perfection, our inherent purity. We keep our awareness always in this high state. With these attitudes of integrity and purity we treat effectively and place new causes in motion relative to the people in our world; we see everybody, all the time, as whole and perfect. In this sense we are a healer; we return in awareness to our original purity and integrity and recognize everyone as whole and perfect. We see everyone in this wondrous world, which we create, as an outpicturing of total wholeness and perfection.

We are our own healer for we put the Law in motion for us. We determine the conditions under which we live; we create all goodness in our life by our thoughts. We enjoy a perfect body, we enjoy perfect health in body and mind by our choice. We heal ourselves as we keep our thoughts always pure; we dwell with all our thoughts on beauty, on abundance, on peace and on harmony.

We may be the catalyst for other people in our world. We show how we use the Law efficiently, beneficially for us. We give examples of our life where we create wholeness by speaking our word. Our entire life is an outpicturing of our use of the Law. By our example we are a channel, we create a change in the consciousness of all people, people who are our creation.

I recognize only one healer: *Me!* I realize that it is done according to my innermost belief.

I heal myself. I speak my word for absolute purity in body, mind and spirit. I visualize a pure, whole and perfect body. I see every organ and function totally in a perfect state. I bless my body and honor it as a temple of the living God. I visualize it as a wonderful divine instrument. I keep my thoughts about it pure; I am the healer for I put the causes in motion of a whole and perfect body.

The Practitioner a Medical/Spiritual Healer

◆

The ability to be so absolutely onepointed in our thought comes through specific training and honest effort on our part. It may seem as though it is not worth the effort because the benefits are often slow in coming.

Why, we may ask, are the benefits slow in coming: the only answer is that any doubt we ever know plays havoc with our installation of the principle in our life.

The Law only knows how to do whatever it is we ask of it. It makes no judgment. The Law, however, can only work on one proposition at a time. So if we say **yes** to one prospect, it says yes to that prospect. If we say **no** to a prospect, the Law says no to that prospect. We are often so variable and so unstable in our thinking that in an instant we may consider numerous conclusions for ourselves.

This is purely a lack of discipline in our lives.

We have been trained to believe the medical doctor will take away our pain and heal our illnesses. As we believe, it is done unto us.

If we were to think the medical doctors could not heal us or take away our pain, this would also be true as it has been time and again in medical history.

Putting the perfect mental thought into power in our lives, standing by that perfect thought, results in an effect so mind boggling and earth shaking that we would never depart from it again.

The only question is, when will we begin our training on this onepointedness.

Think how everyone of us could be grand musicians, but how few of us train for this skill which brings so much joy into our world.

Something so obvious and proven that it works yet it is not carried through. It is therefore easy to see why something so mystical and shrouded in secrecy gains so little of our real attention.

The introspective path in spiritual study develops masters. Smile! ∞

Theme Eleven

THE PRACTITIONER A MINISTER

*E*very practitioner is a minister.

A minister is one who practices the art of sharing sensitivity with humanity guiding each one on the highest path of existence. The minister may offer the sacraments of the church and the minister may work closely with individuals who have come to respect and trust his judgment, but in the last analysis, the true minister is one who is the balancer in the lives of his creation.

Smile!

How seldom do we think of a minister being a person who has created his flock. Seldom do we recognize that each minister has created himself and all those who people his world. This is readily seen in church goers. A minister draws (we say creates) about him those who are harmonious with his teaching and his sharing techniques. When that minister leaves, the flock disperses. When a new minister comes the new pastor creates his own flock—some may be the same as before—but by enlarge most are newly coming for this sharer.

Be not surprised that each minister has created the flock and parishioners whom are most like him. So, we can see that no matter how grand or lowly our calling may be, we are the creator therein.

Assuming the title and mantle of minister we come to a further responsibility. We are trusted by our flock as their priest. We are indentured as their creators and insofar as this is true, our task could be greater, but truly is not. All we have to do is to be ourselves, remain true to ourselves, love ourselves, and all whom we serve will reap the harvest of our creation of them as ourselves—and all is good and very good.

Read here how these professional practitioners and ministers define their work:

The practitioner as a minister is comprehensively delineated by the Rev Dr Ellen Jermini as she spells out the rules of conduct, the code of ethics, and the vows of commitment made by individuals who align themselves in the professional status of minister through the Church of God Unlimited and in the training of the University of

Healing and its Ministerial Program. While this training is noteworthy, it merely defines a professional minister and his outreach. We as practitioners define our ministry even more subjectively, for it is an inner thing first. It is an inner knowingness that first we create ourselves, then we create those in our world and our universe. Insofar as this is our course and procedure, we have a magnificent responsibility to our creation.

We Are Balancers of Life

We are born on this planet Earth to be free spirits, to make our choices in life and have fun doing it. We practitioners may dedicate our life as ministers, counselors, teachers, spiritual messengers—by our own choice—studying diligently the principles of life and standing for them strongly like a power rock. We live as a perfect viable example for ourselves and our created world and competently serve as ministers, as representatives of truth. We may go out in the world to share our belief, our indwelling divinity, our God presence.

As ministers of the Church of God Unlimited, we have finished our studies, the undergraduate course of the University of Healing *The Art And Science Of Wholeness* and know perfectly the basis of the great teachings: we know the philosophy

The Practitioner a Minister

of life. Through sincerity in our choice, we decide to serve as a practitioner/minister to make each life we touch more joyous, more glorious. We live in the light and love of truth and let each being on Earth ignite his own light using the symbolical church ceremonies.

We perform wedding, baptism or funeral services confirming ourselves as fulfilled beings. We bless the new born baby with words of love and whisper in its ears the wisdom of life. We share with the bride and the groom in a commemorated wedding service the true enjoyment of life, the pure motive of sharing in marriage and understand the boundless experience in oneness as the everlasting light and love of a perfect marriage. We bless their life, we love them.

We are practitioners, ordained ministers and honor the highest ecclesiastical recognition given to us as a priest, or administrator of the church. The rite of ordination through which we commit ourselves to serve as a minister stands as the key to ethical standards by which we live and function as representatives of truth. We are practitioners/ministers, *we are the balancer of life*, we recognize the purity within all men, we live in the awareness of being God, that all is God.

The purpose of being a minister, says the Rev Dr Stefan Strässle, *is to practice our own belief and be what we are!* In this simple definition, Dr Strässle has given power to the concept of everyman being his selfcreator. For everyman the world in which he lives is his creation totally. In his illustration from the county jail where he performed a wedding, Professor Strässle pictures for the reader an event memorable to him and everyone else and in that creation he describes how absolutely free and responsive everyone was to HIS CREATION!

A Minister Creates About Him Expressions of Perfection

*A*s practitioners we practice our belief and conviction. As practitioners we live who and what we are. We live according to principle: the Law of cause and effect. We practice the Law and achieve everything we desire in our life and in the lives of our friends who come to us to strengthen their own belief about themselves.

Now, what is a minister? A minister performs the duties of a practitioner for a minister creates his world filled with joy, harmony and love. A minister creates about him expressions of perfection in all avenues of life, a reflection of himself.

As ministers we perform the special duties for our ministry and congregation like baptisms, funerals, weddings and ordinations. Doing these wonderful tasks, we as ministers add our special thoughts and blessings to the rituals—through our being successful practitioners—and empower the whole ceremony to outpicture an uplifting, spiritually illuminating experience.

This reminds me of an experience while performing a wedding ceremony in a visiting room of a county jail, where the groom served his time for a law violation. The bride and the groom were required to sit in two different rooms facing each other through a small glass window. The bride and I, as the performing minister, and the groom had telephones and each one a receiver to be able to communicate to perform this outstanding wedding ceremony.

It was, despite the unusual and quite limiting circumstances, a very, very special wedding ceremony for I as the minister gave my total heart, my absolute love, my overwhelming joy into this special event and made it—by my own consciousness—an unforgettable, joyous and sparkling moment for the bride and groom and for everyone else present. The bride said: *It is the vibrations of love, oneness and joy exuding from the entire ceremony that make this wedding the most special day of my life.* The outer circumstances seemed forgotten, so much were we all absorbed with the beauty of this event.

This is the magnificent thing about being both a minister and a practitioner. We can practice our belief as practitioners in an even wider field and touch the lives of so many glorious souls, however always reminding us of the purpose why we perform any action: to practice our own belief and be what we are!

The work of meditation and sharing with friends through the work of the church ministry is defined beautifully by Professor Ingeborg Puchert. The impressive beginning which she infuses into our consciousness is where the Rev Puchert says: *We live by the teachings of the master teacher within*, defines the perfect work of a minister and of a practitioner at full sway in his field of expression.

Our Words Are Sticky and Stay in the Consciousness

*W*e are ordained ministers of the Church of God Unlimited. We live by the teachings of the master teacher within. We thoroughly listen to the voice of that inner teacher and follow it as we practice unconditional love and understanding. We are fantastic beings in doing the work of both the minister and the practitioner.

We feel guided from within and follow this inner calling. We accept this task and know consciously that we are prepared for the work of practitioner and minister. We are inspired from within to teach, preach and heal. Through every word we speak and share with the congregation we let flow the beautiful affirmations about the divine reality of our beingness.

The Practitioner a Minister

Our parishioners come to us for Sunday services. We take this opportunity and work as them on a pure consciousness. Out of our heart we let flow the stream of lovely givingness and share pure thoughts and ideas of a fulfilled life.

We meditate and prepare ourselves for sharing our ideas of who and what we are with the friends. We have a glorious feeling of oneness with the congregation. We listen to the heart of the friends and experience oneness with the universal energy.

In this feeling of oneness we experience healings. We experience the effect of our good thoughts in our life as in the life of the friends. Our words are sticky and stay in the consciousness of the friends and in this way we create in the friends the broader view of their reality.

We work actively for our church and reap the harvest in the material gifts we receive from the community. We notice the effect of the universal principles we teach. We are delighted in the love and harmony coming to us through our friends.

An introspective lady is the Rev Dr Katarina Suter as she defines the role of the practitioner as a minister. She says: *We realize that every practitioner living his life among people acts also as a minister; however, as a good minister we are a practitioner first, which means that our purpose of life is to be who and what we are!* Succinct and comprehensive. The master touch at work here.

The Pure Socratic Teacher

As a practitioner we practice and live what we know as true about ourselves. We express all the love and peace and harmony which a spiritual master is. We live for the sake of being a master fulfilled within ourselves and through ourselves. We are the light in our world and illumine each scene as we put our attention on it.

In living as this perfect light we are a pure mirror to all the people in our world. They see in us the truth about themselves and have the desire to know more about this perfect light or attitude about life which we express. This is where we as a practitioner enter the field of a minister.

Here is an example. I am at the funeral of my grandfather. My heart is filled with joy in the awareness of this great man who is a living example of wisdom in my life. I feel a great happiness in my heart and radiate the oneness which is without the awareness of death or separation. An aunt comes to me and asks me about the reason of my happiness at a day like this—a funeral. I explain to her my experience of oneness as my grandfather and that he is more alive within me than ever.

I talk about the illusion of the body and the reality of the eternal divine within each being. Through the question of my aunt I as a practitioner fulfill the work of a minister.

Whenever we explain the reason of a certain expression in our life we do the work of a minister.

Whenever we share our experience of life with another being we do the work of a minister, which is the function of a catalyzer, for every word we speak catalyzes something in our fellowman and confirms to ourselves what we know within ourselves.

A good way of answering any question is the Socratic method. Whenever someone comes and asks about the reason for our happiness and joy in life we ask the questioner why he thinks he sees these virtues in us. A good minister lets the people answer their own questions, for an answer given by ourselves tends to be meaningless.

With this recognition we realize that every practitioner living his life among people acts also as a minister; however, as a good minister we are a practitioner first, which means that our purpose of life is to be who we are!

Here we find two definitions: a public minister and a private minister. The Rev Dr Sylvia Maria Enz intellectually lays the ground for comprehensive awareness of just how a public minister, a private minister and a practitioner function together as one being. While Dr Enz lays hold to the symbol of being a servant, this symbol returns again and again to the servant to the Law, servant to the program, servant to a philosophy or belief. These are interesting and important considerations.

We Are the Servants of What We Believe

A minister is someone who officially represents a belief. It is someone who can conduct services which are the link in the act where he shares his deep understanding with people who come into his world because they are attracted by what he preaches. In the first definition of the dictionary a minister is—a servant.

A servant on the other hand is someone who is devoted to another, to a cause, to a creed. That leads us immediately to the point where the practitioner is a minister.

We as practitioners know that we are the allness of God, the purity of the universe, the creative cause of all—simply the most wonderful being on the face of the Earth.

As practitioners we know the truth about ourselves and practice to stay in this awareness of truth each moment of our beingness. We create friends in our world challenging us to look at appearances and we see beyond, right to the center of beingness and recognize the same wonderful being as we are, we see the pure reflection of ourselves. We are the servants of what we believe.

To be a servant of course means to give. We as practitioners give and share our awareness of who and what we are with everybody who enters our world without expectation of something in return.

The Practitioner a Minister

In a way we are in the same position as parents toward their child. The child came into their world because it wants to be a part of their way of living, their way of thinking, their way of sharing, to be as a grown up a wonderful living example of truth in his own world.

The parents are the servant of this child on the way to its inner awareness. They unconditionally enfold it in their love, their expectation of the highest and best; they recognize its perfection regardless of apparent struggles and difficulties. While they give unconditionally to that child they are all what they give. That is the reward of being a parent.

We as ministers are like the parents. We give unconditionally to everybody who enters our world on their way to inner awareness.

We as ministers may be aware of the appearances of our friends but like the parents we see the complete, the fulfilled being in each one. We see it done. We create our friends in our life to keep the awareness of truth about ourselves alive.

We as ministers are the confirmation of our belief. We are the living example for ourselves—and then all the world sees us like this and recognizes itself in us as we recognize ourselves in them. We are the servants of each other.

The act of sharing is one of the most rewarding experiences of the ministry, states the Rev Dr Ilse Wenk, director of the Worldwide Healing Ministry of the Church of God Unlimited. Having a full understanding of the processes through which each individual works to achieve their ultimate goal of oneness in spiritual things, Dr Wenk works with her creation to open the door to their own inner state of awareness and to remain in this blissful realm.

The Voice Within the True Language of Our Beingness

We know that preaching is the most important ministry of the church. We work closely together with all friends who come to talk to us or to listen to us.

Our main work is that we dedicate our life sharing with others: to find the own way. We are all healing channels. All who come to us go through the channel of spiritual healing.

We as practitioners/ministers give a service with absolute faith and expectation, with absolute love. We are the instruments of God and think only good thoughts and speak good words and do good deeds. We use the Law of cause and effect to manifest that which is the birthright of every individual. The Law of cause and effect is the only Law in the universe. We are responsible for every thought we think because every thought is a cause for whatever we experience. Therefore we take full responsibility for our thoughts, words and actions.

The Practitioner a Minister

We as ministers are totally concerned with our state of awareness. We recognize that the world in which we live is pure and perfect. Our principle function is to practice spiritual purity and spiritual mind treatment.

We share and are in contact with the father within. We listen constantly to the voice within which is the true language of our beingness.

We have a prayer group. In this prayer group we speak our word individually for all our friends who come for healing treatment. We apply cause and effect, love, prayer, awareness, knowingness to the awareness of the body, mind and spirit. God is the only source of healing.

A friend came to me who wanted to put a new cause into motion. She asked me which cause I would suggest. I told the friend that the cause is an individual creation which is found by each one alone. I worked it out in a significant talk with the friend who left happily because she had found the cause herself. To be a practitioner/minister is a rewarding work.

Practice, practice, practice: this is the thesis of the Rev Dr Robert Rettel. To know the Law and the principle is beneficial only as it is exercised and used. Being a minister and a practitioner for Dr Rettel means seeing all his creation as perfect as he is, seeing all of his world in its highest potential expressed. This is done with friend and/or family, all one.

The Minister Speaks as a Practitioner at All Times

*W*e always see everyone from the highest viewpoint; we recognize in everyone their innate beauty and purity. All the time we see with eyes of perfection. We recognize every condition as whole and perfect. This is the highest calling for everybody; we recognize absolutely everyone as pure from the very beginning. We see perfection in all; we dwell with our onepointed attention on perfection. All the time we practice the truth about ourselves and our world. We see purity in our entire universe. We see purity in all. We are pure.

To everybody in our world we say: *I see me perfect. Now, my friend I see you whole and perfect; I see you enjoying your original purity and integrity. Together we recognize your innate wholeness and perfection. Together we put a new cause in motion on your behalf.*

I see you whole and perfect, I see you pure.

Together we put all our thoughts on the indwelling divinity and recognize but one power in all.

We show our friend the right use of the Law by examples of our life.

Whatever we see in the inner we continue and see as the truth. We see absolutely every situation as whole and perfect. We put the Law in motion on our behalf and for the entire universe.

The Practitioner a Minister

In the first place we are a practitioner. We recognize our highest *duty* is as a practitioner of truth. We plant the seeds of truth, all the time we speak our word for wholeness and perfection.

We are a practitioner. We see the truth in every situation and in everyone. We dwell with all our thoughts on purity, on harmony, on peace and on abundance.

I get a letter from my sister where I read about a health problem. I speak my word for wholeness and perfection. I recognize the truth. I see her in a perfect state. I meet her recently during her stay in Luxembourg and I hear about her perfect health.

◆

There is no difference between being a minister and being a practitioner. Each lives what he believes about himself and practices it continuously in every moment of his life. The minister is more trained in depth in certain areas of interpersonal relationships and public speaking, business management, and all other areas in which he must perform.

The true minister goes out and shares what he is with his world. The true minister knows no limitation except those he creates for himself, for the true minister is constantly expressing what he believes about himself and all the world is a reflection for him of this belief and of these convictions.

At all times, the minister is a practitioner, and the practitioner is a minister! ∞

Theme Twelve

THE SECRET OF MIRACLES

A miracle is an event that takes place beneficially to us serendipitously.

Some might say they sought after the miracle and looked for that good in their lives but truly it was not not sought after: Negative thoughts refuted it.

But, let us get back to the miracle word itself. A miracle is defined as something which takes place which does not necessarily come about because of some effort put into achieving it on our part. This is utterly false. **We MAKE every miracle happen**. We specifically put the cause in motion which results in any miracle. It may be serendipitous from the point of view that we were not confident in the principle, but nonetheless the principle works.

The Secret of Miracles

If a child in school does not believe in the principle of mathematics, yet he consistently uses it, the principle WORKS regardless that the youngster believes in it or not. The universal Law of cause and effect functions in like manner. The LAW is unmindful of whether we believe in it or not. The Law has no emotions that say you did not believe in me therefore I will not function—the Law just does our bidding. The key is in the bidding of the Law. Are we sincere and do we remain onepointed in the establishment of the Law to accomplish our choice! The results indicate whether we have done so or not.

The SECRET OF MIRACLES is that onepointed utilization of the principle through the Law of cause and effect, brings results. Multipointed use of the Law brings multiresponses. That is the secret!

The most effective proof that miracles are not a secret is in the demonstration of the principle. Dr Ellen Jermini illustrates here the use of the Law, the expression of the *Secret Of Miracles*, most effectively in her working with a student who had little, put the principle to work innocently and eagerly, and benefitted in results beyond belief. Eager onepointedness manifests in miracles instantly!

The Miracle Millionaire

*H*ow often we read in newspapers or hear broadcast in the news of radio or television about miraculous events happening in the world and we remain firm exclaiming: *How lucky!* We practitioners know that luck or often so called destiny is simply being in charge of our life. We are responsible beings, responsible basically—and that is all that it needs—in our thoughts, words and deeds; we use the great Law, the Law of cause and effect in a beneficial way, for us a desirable way.

I recall an exciting story which surprised many friends of mine. One of our students had decided to take the undergraduate course of the University of Healing. He had heard that miracles happen to those who take the course and he was ready to change his life. However, he faced an apparent *problem*. His monthly income was so little that he promised us a weekly rate payment based on the small amount he could afford. We worked with him and accepted his offer knowing that the pupil's eagerness in being a diligent and disciplined pupil was the warranty for his success. In following the requirements of the cause, he quickly learned how to enjoy miracles, how to live a wonderful life; he learned how to use the principle, how to put causes into motion. He demonstrated the winner he always was!

This man became a millionaire, yes his life completely changed from one minute to the other, he was the lucky one, he won in lotto, he won $1,000,000. He later told us that he bought the lotto ticket following his inner voice, *his first thought*, while visualizing himself with a big amount of money in his hands and knowing that it was done. He acted with faith, he acted convinced about the result, he felt worthy of accepting a miracle happening. He loved this idea, he stood firm on this idea.

As we use the Law of cause and effect wisely and beneficially, as we take charge of our everyday life, we know that the secrets of miracles are the wisdom of following our intuitive self, our heart, following the secret voice of truth. The truth about ourselves is unchangeable, everlasting. The truth is that we are God, that we are all, that we are unlimited. We are the abundance of the universe, we are the one source of wealth and health, we are the creators and masters of our world. We alone perform the miracles in life and know the world's secrets of miracles: we think our thought and we let it happen. We practitioners know it is done.

Miracles happen because they are expected to happen. Miracles take place because they are possible. Miracles are a common occurrence because we are aware of them and DO NOT TAKE THEM FOR GRANTED. Dr Stefan Strässle in his illustration shows that he was unconcerned that the machine, over which he was asked to be a successful effective beneficial expectant practitioner in his mind, functioned. He did not question why it did not function for others. He wrapped the room and the machine in **his** white light of love and the principle did what *HE EXPECTED IT TO DO*! Is that so strange, hardly, a practitioner knows of the Law, how it works, and puts that principle into action.

The Recalcitrant Printer

Miracles bring excitement, enthusiasm and joy to everyone. Our hearts are filled with happiness when miracles happen and make our dreams come true. We admire individuals performing miracles because they accomplish the expected, the possible. We look at miracles in total wonderment because they touch the real us within us and make us feel that everything is possible, that we are unlimited and free in our ultimate nature.

We all have experienced miracles. Everyday we practitioners—and every person on the face of the Earth (is a practitioner)—perform miracles. In fact everything we do is a real miracle. We get up in the morning and start walking on the floor. It is a real miracle that we are able to do this. It is a miracle that we do not sink through the floor down into the earth! We are able to perfectly and harmoniously walk on the floor because we call the floor solid and *totally believe that it is so*. This is a real miracle!!!

To walk on solid ground is just as much a miracle as it is to walk on water or to walk over fire. The secret to perform a miracle is always our

The Secret of Miracles

belief, our inner conviction, our absolute knowingness that what we choose to perform *is already done*. We call water solid rock and there we go walking on water just as easy as we do on the ground—a miracle. We call fire cool wet moss and we walk over the fire without burning our feet—a miracle!

An example of a recalcitrant printer demonstrates this principle effectively:

I am called in an office where a computer printer is improperly functioning. Outwardly the printer seems to be OK. All the lights indicating power are turned on, the ribbon is inserted, the fonts are placed in the machine perfectly. Everything seems perfect! It is really a mystery why the machine performs as it does. Everyone at the office—all computer specialists—try to make the machine function again but they are unsuccessful and finally leave it to me to do the job. Before I enter the office I speak my word that this printer is functioning perfectly right now. I surround it by my white light of love. Then I enter the room. I am shown the printer and give the necessary commands to the computer to print a document. Everyone is anxious to see what happens . . . a miracle!!! The printer functions perfectly.

This is a simple demonstration of how we practitioners perform miracles. The secret—as always—lies in the onepointed visualization of the effect we choose to experience. It is always our onepointed belief, our inner conviction, our knowingness from our heart which sets the Law of cause and effect into motion to achieve any goal. We each one are miracle people and now know it in our hearts and create miracles consciously everyday. It is a glorious experience.

We create miracles by our thought, declares Dr Ingeborg Puchert. She directs our attention to the one-pointed thought, consistent with every effective practitioner, to set the Law of cause and effect in motion for beneficial results. Most people have no idea how many miracles they experience in life. If every being on the face of the globe would take a little booklet and list—every day—everything they consider a miracle, they would find in a short time instead of relisting the same old miracles, new ones would begin to appear more and more until they would have no time to list them because they happened so frequently.

Thoughts Bounce Out Miracles

*W*e live in a wonderful world, a world of our own creation. We create by thought and take responsibility for every thought we think and each word we speak. For every thought we think we experience an effect and that effect we call a miracle. We consciously put causes in motion. The effects of these causes we call manifestations, the manifestations of the desires we have for ourselves and our world.

We say we create by thought and know that whatever thought we think is kept eternally in the memory of the universal mind. Through our mind we have access to the infinite record of thoughts stored in the universe. We call it the universal mind, the one mind that is! In the universal mind we experience knowledge. As we tune into our universal mind, the one mind, we achieve through disciplined thinking, onepointedness on our thoughts.

We clearly and definitely know that the miracles we experience in our world are the effect of the Law of cause and effect. We practitioners work without using secrets, secret rites or secret formulas. We openly proclaim who we are and what we think is the truth about ourselves. We freely teach the truth and know the truth of the God presence within us. Whatever happens to us or in our world we accept as the effect of the thoughts we think. In the effect we see the relationship between the spoken word and the miracle.

One of the miracles I experienced: For my meditation I sit outside on the trunk of an old tree. It gets windy. I speak my word of peace and experience that while the wind blows in the areas next to me, I am surrounded by total calm. I am one as all and I am in control of my thoughts and world.

We come up with the simple conclusion that we are the universal knowingness. We as the omniscience dispense wisdom and knowledge in our world without holding back anything. We are the harmony of this concept and flow peacefully with this ideal.

We bring forth from within the material manifestation. We bring forth conditions of weather, temperature, cleanliness. We keep our life and world in a balanced condition, the effect of our own inner balance. All these wonderful effects we call miracles. We recognize that we are the cause and in the effects we see outpictured the miracle of our own being, for we are it. We are called miraculous beings. We call miracle the return to the original purity and perfection of the physical body.

Truly we excuse ourselves from being aware of the miracles which take place in our life and experience. We do this in saying that the things that happen are not miracles. Such as the birth of a baby, the development of the human body, the translation of food into energy and substance as we eat, the dropping of pills on the bathroom floor when we for an instant think of the possibility as has done Dr Katarina Suter. To enjoy more miracles take credit for the ones you are daily experiencing. The flood has just begun.

We All Love Miracles

*W*e all love miracles and we are all eager to know the secret behind each miracle. We call an experience a miracle when we are without understanding of how a circumstance enters our world. As a practitioner we know that the secret of any miracle is the use of the Law of cause and effect. The socalled miracle is but a onepointed thought in our mind which manifests. This seems to take all the excitement out of a miracle. The real miracle lies in the training of our thought.

We call a miracle: the instant manifestation of a thought. A thought instantly manifests in our world as we train ourselves in onepointedness, humility, discipline, dedication, determination and diligence.

Here I give an example of an instant manifestation of a thought in my life. I walk into the bathroom and take a little white pill out of a plastic box. The box is full of white pills. For the fraction of a second I think: How would that be if the box would slip out of my hand and the pills roll all over the floor. I take the pill out of the box, screw the cover back on and hold it at the cover to put it back into the cupboard. The cover comes off the box and the pills roll all over the bathroom floor. In this moment I know that this is a miracle, an instant manifestation of my thought.

Through an experience like this one we realize the power of our thought and the importance of the training of our thought so that we are absolutely aware of each thought we think for each thought is a manifestation in our world.

A very effective training of our thoughts is to think, speak and live in the first person, present tense and positive.

We are the creator of our world and stand for it. We look at everything from the center of the world which is ourselves. This is living in the first person. We master each situation in our life in the now. We are without past or future, all happens in the now. We speak our word for love, peace and harmony in our life now. This is living in the present tense. Each thought we think and each word we speak is absolutely positive. We look at our creation and see the positive in it. We empower the positive, we dwell upon the positive and therefore experience a positive life. This is living positive.

The secret of miracles is simple. It is our conscious use of the Law of cause and effect and the awareness that we are the sole creator of our world.

Medical science says the remission of disease or illness from the body is usually unexpected and certainly most desired. Sometimes it goes away and sometimes it merely goes into hiding to raise its doleful head at another unwanted time in our life. Dr Sylvia Maria Enz says these spontaneous returns to one's original purity and integrity are the real miracles of life. There is no expectation that it will take place and none that it will not, it is just that the cause was put into motion and the effect came about. The miracle is that we cannot see how really effective our utilization of principle and our purposeful use of the Law is.

Claiming and Accepting Results in Miracles

The spontaneous, instantaneous return to one's original purity and integrity (healing) is called a miracle. We all know of happenings like that in our lives or in the lives of our friends. What happens in that moment that brings that miracle about?

The easiest way to describe this is an illustration out of my life and the experience of what I call my daily miracles, the blessings of a wonderful day.

I experience a pain in my arm in the evening during my meditation/introspection time so I speak my word for peace of body and mind and instantly I feel how my body enters the state of blissful peace. In this calmness of mind and body I feel an absolute wellbeing of body and mind—including my arm. As I come out of my meditation this feeling stays with me.

Another time as I feel a similar situation in my body I apply the same technique. During my busy work schedule I tell myself that I am at peace and go with my attention to that inner place of light and calmness and I feel myself in the same peacefulness and wellbeing.

This blessing we call a miracle happens to each of us. Whenever we are in harmony with our divine self, with our inner reality we feel at peace. We feel the goodness and joy of life filling every area of our life. Every little thing in our world radiates this awareness and we truly live in bliss, our wholeness and perfection which is now a miracle and our reality.

Whenever we step out of the balance which is our true self and speak our word to claim this oneness once again we call it a miracle. When we look at a miracle from this point of view we realize that a miracle has no secret or any special trick about it. It is merely claiming and *accepting* our reality.

We as practitioners know who and what we are and we live in the miracle (effect) of this awareness. We live in the constant miracle of our authenticity. We are perfect. We are whole and perfect now. We are our own miracle as we are the creator of our world.

When we can visualize all of the little things in our life and know that each *little thing* is truly a miracle, then we will begin to understand what Dr Ilse Wenk is describing to us here. She tells of the numerous times we set in motion the miracle producer *Law of cause and effect* in asking or thinking about finding something which is not usual to find. She illustrates the concept of seeking a word in the dictionary and then serendipitously opening the dictionary directly at the word sought. A miracle, quite so! Dr Wenk relates this as something that just happens and so it is.

Some Real Miracles

*M*iracles happen to us all day, without our being aware of them. One miracle is when I look up a word in the dictionary which has 95,000 words and by opening the book I am already at the word. This is indeed a real miracle.

The secret of a miracle is to let lose and let go and let God. As for instance when we are relaxed without wanting something, just letting *it* happen, *it happens*. And then by being aware of it brings about a miraculous result we utilize time and again.

For us each day of life is a most beautiful miracle. Sometimes we are absorbed in looking at a flower. In a single blossom we find innumerable petals. And the scent of the blossoming flower is so wonderful. This is really a miracle.

When we wake up in the morning and are aware of life we recognize all life is a miracle. We walk around in our body, the temple of the living God and move purposefully. That, too, is a miracle.

We say: *Every organ, action and function of my body is absolutely perfect right now,* and it is. That is a miracle, let alone our skin, such a vast organ, functioning so beautifully we say, this is a miracle.

People often look for miracles without being aware that the whole of life is a miracle and that no secrets are involved in what we call miracles.

When I look at my body, the temple of the living God, I say to myself *what a miracle!*

Our life is an open book. Every movement we make is seen and perceived by our outer and inner eye.

We all live with one universal Law. The same Law for all of us. This Law is called the Law of cause and effect. This Law of cause and effect is a miracle. It does exactly what we think. Sounds funny but it is true. Each one of our thoughts is a cause with which the Law of cause and effect outpictures every moment of our life who and what we are. Our life is omniscient, onepointed and aware.

The innate God power is the real actor through the Law of cause and effect, points out Dr Robert Rettel. Just as the rule of mathematics is not the principle of mathematics itself, so the Law of cause and effect is not that which it effects or not that which effects it. Everything in our life is a miracle, says Dr Rettel and it is up to us to fully enjoy it.

The Real Actor

We are the creator of our entire universe. We create every situation, every condition in our world. We have at our disposition a great present:

The Law of cause and effect. Whatever we give into the Law we get back. With every thought we put a cause in motion, with every thought we actuate the Law and create a result in our world.

We create wondrous conditions in our life; we recognize all these conditions as the working of the Law. We have a whole and perfect body which we recognize truly as a miracle. We realize that our body is really a great instrument with all its various organs, vessels, functions and actions, with the brain as the operator, the supervisor of the whole organism. We recognize our body with which we perform more functions than in the best equipped laboratory, as a great miracle. Our body is an outpicturing of the thoughts that we have about it. We think of a marvelous body and we enjoy perfect health. All day long we think very highly of our body; we know it is as a perfect God machine.

We recognize all the events in our world as the result of the Law of cause and effect. We think our thought and recognize the Law as the actor upon our thoughts. We think pure thoughts, thoughts of wholeness and perfection and we experience pure conditions. We recognize all as the working of the Law, as the result of our thoughts.

Everything in our life is a *miracle*, a wondrous, beautiful, fantastic experience that we create through our pure thoughts. We recognize in our entire universe one power, one presence. The divine reality within us. This innate God power is the real actor, the true performer of all the *miracles* in our entire universe. We think the thoughts of God; we recognize all our universe as a divine, whole and perfect idea, and we experience *miracles*, wondrous, peaceful, joyous and harmonious events in our life.

I watch my thoughts; I think thoughts of wholeness and perfection; I think pure thoughts about my work. I see joy in my work with the computer; I visualize it as interesting; I think harmonious relationships. I experience miracles, the wonders of positive thinking: I enjoy harmony, peace, beauty and goodness at work.

◆

Into every life miracles flood out in greater and greater measure as a giant river gathering up waters from the feeder rivers and creeks that blend into the great father of the waters. We are seemingly unaware of this influx of water. We look at each pastoral rivulet and revel in its beauty and in its purpose. Then the moment comes that we see flooding out at the delta all of the soil which has been gathered during its journey. Then we are aware of just what has taken place. The miracle of removal of tons upon millions of tons of alluvium from the land and deposited into the apparently useless delta lands and the sea.

Miracles work much in this same manner for each of us. Little by little the functioning of life goes on. We eat and our bodies grow. We bless our world and we are blessed by it in return. We think positive thoughts and enjoy a world of positive expression. Or, we give out pessimism and wonder why nothing seems to work out for us. We give out unbeneficial virtues and reap the reward of their sewing. All is our choice.

May we ever be mindful of the manner in which the waters flowing over the land gather topsoil and toss it into the sea. This same thing affects us perfectly when we choose to be aware of how the system works.

From tiny specks of topsoil a new delta is created. From tiny thoughts consistently held in consciousness come great miracles which bless our life infinitely. ∞

Theme Thirteen

THE PRACTITIONER'S CHARISMA

*E*very being has a dynamic self that radiates out from within which either repels or attracts his world. This attraction is not really attraction in the sense of magnetizing the world to him. It is more in a symbolic sense *like attracts like*. A happy smile *attracts* smiles, a frown frowns. More realistically the inner self we are is not so much attracted to us but *reflected back from others in our world*.

All the world about us is our reflection. A practitioner knows this categorically, unquestioningly, and so having the allness within determines that to reflect back anything that must first be shone out from within.

The Practitioner's Charisma

The charisma of a practitioner is his competence in knowing who and what he is and using his exceptional awareness or ability to shine it out so it is reflected back to him from those in his world as devotion and loyalty.

The practitioner is a master of knowing what from within he will shine out to purposefully create his world about him utilizing the dynamics of his charisma to affect his choices. His influence and impact are all important. Whatever a practitioner sees, regardless it may appear to be created or caused by others, it is his creation—his affectation—his charismatic response or reflection in his world.

The oft used phrase: *Physician Heal Thyself* refers to practitioners primarily. First the practitioner chooses from within his harmonious aura, his distinctive quality, and all his world reflects it in return. If a practitioner sees those with whom he practices as *they* may see themselves, he is on that level. However, this is impossible, for a practitioner can only see all from his inner sun, his inner charisma!

Dr Ellen Jermini defines *charisma* as **mental attitude**! She calls it a secret because it is commonly believed to be a condition available to only a few. It is often the simplest illustration which is the most impressive in revealing basic truths. Abbot Jermini demonstrates effective charismatic expressions.

Charisma/Attitude

Whenever we talk about the charismatic radiance of a person, we practitioners know that we mean the aura of this person, we mean the special atmosphere we sense being in this person's presence. We say it is a joy, it is a pleasure, it is so special to stay close to this person exuding excellence, exuding peace and harmony. We simply feel good staying in the charisma of this lovely being and we search out their company.

But what is the secret such a charismatic person expresses for himself! We practitioners know that this secret of life is our mental attitude, that all is attitude; we create our life through our thoughts, through our attitude about ourselves and our world. We exude vibrations around us which shine forth as and in the appearance of ourselves a divine-human being, which shine forth through the illusion of our body, which are like the sun reflecting brilliance and power in our total being, by our choice.

To give an example I remember an optometrist I visit from time to time. Whenever I enter the little room to sit down ready for my eye examination, I find a radiant person standing in front of me. I look into a big smiling face, the young doctor's face, and with joy in his heart he says: *Ellen, how good to see you, you always make my day, you are such a cheerful, happy person, I like your powerful positive attitude about life.*

I smile back to the doctor and say, *But doctor, you see what you are, I am your reflection, you are*

The Practitioner's Charisma

joy, you are happiness, you practice this positive attitude yourself.

We both laugh and feel good about each other.

Yes, we practitioners live a happy life. Our happiness, our inner joy of knowing who and what we are determine our excellence of being. We love and respect ourselves as divine beings, we live in the nonjudgmental attitude of unconditional givingness, total givingness from and to ourselves. We live in the light of inner wisdom, we live in the realm of our God presence. Living in the faith, the belief *yes* the knowingness of the truth about ourselves, knowing that we are the omniscience, omnipresence, omnipotence, that we are God, the allness, we stand up for our uniqueness of being, we stand up for what we really are.

Through this knowingness we live our charisma, we exude powerful vibrations which demonstrate our world and define ourselves as that what we think about ourselves, what, indeed, we are. We think we are joy, happiness, health and wealth, we think we are peace, harmony and love as we KNOW that what we think is true; it is our charisma, the charisma of a wise practitioner.

The joy of being a practitioner is that we at all times remain who we are and what we are. We know our divinity and our oneness as all. In doing this we, as pure love, (create) have reflected back in our world an exact duplicate of our thinking, our seeing, our acting. Hence, if we are loving, thoughtful, sincere, dedicated, happy people, so are all in our world. If not, whatever our world is, it is our reflection. Dr Stefan Strässle insists: *We express our charisma every moment of our lives.*

A Reflection, Under All Circumstances

*C*harisma means the special, supernatural, inspiring power all have innate within our very being. We all have this charismatic power within us. We practitioners train ourselves to express charisma every moment of our lives.

Charisma expresses itself in our being as a pure reflection of the love we have towards ourselves. We practitioners love and respect ourselves completely. We live and express selflove, selfrespect and selfconfidence at all times, under all circumstances.

To love ourselves is one of the most beautiful and thrilling things we can ever experience. It is an overwhelmingly happy, joyous, free, peaceful, unlimited and harmonious experience. Through selflove we touch the divine within us. In fact, selflove is the key to being the absolute master of our life and affairs.

The selflove which is our charisma is a very important virtue for us practitioners while we harmoniously work with our friends who ask for prayer treatment. Expressing charisma creates about us a vibration of peace, confidence and love.

Every friend entering our charismatic aura immediately feels at home and visions his world, life, experiences from a perfectly balanced point of view. Very often the *problems* with which friends come to us practitioners are immediately turned into solutions because of the peace, balance, harmony and love they sense about us.

This is the beautiful thing about us practitioners being charismatic: we work as catalyzers and present the solutions by just being our wonderful selves.

This reminds me of a talk I had with a ladyfriend. I was invited to a party at her boyfriend's apartment. I sat and talked with several people, however, I said little and was more of an observer that night. The next morning I prepared the breakfast together with her and shared some beautiful ideas about positive thinking and the beauty that life offers to those who choose to see it. In the middle of our talking she suddenly gives me a big bear hug, saying: *I just love to be close to you. Whenever I am near you I feel absolutely at peace. I feel the love and harmony of your being and it is always a wonderful experience to have you here.* This is what the charisma of us practitioners does to our world.

To express charisma is a most exciting experience. It is the noble outpicturing of our inner being. We live the charismatic power from the center of our hearts and include it in all avenues of our glorious lives.

In the presence of the practitioner we feel uplifted, this is our charisma, according to Dr Ingeborg Puchert. Whatever we are we shine out charismatically. Then, since all of the universe is a mirror, whatever we think about ourselves is reflected back to us impersonally, vigorously and perfectly. Professor Puchert reveals this as her audience responds to her personal magnetism, or better charisma, reflecting to her the enthusiasm of her presentation.

Charisma, the Light Within

*W*e meet a person and feel a stream of magic about his physical appearance. This is the charisma of a practitioner who practices what he believes about himself. We are attracted by the evident enthusiasm and joy sparkling out of this being. *In the presence of the practitioner we feel uplifted.* We stand in front of a source of energy. This spiritual energy we call the inner light, the everlasting light. We see it shining forth powerfully, delighting those about him.

We know that the reward of the spiritual work in our own consciousness is recognizing the inner light of us as practitioners. We live charisma in an exemplary way. The discipline and integrity of our thinking is rule number one for us practitioners. This is the fundamental base of the exemplary way of living of the practitioner. Once this high state of consciousness, of inner awareness is achieved, it is eagerly kept up. This means being in total control of our own mental household.

An example of how I experience charisma: I am invited to talk to a group of people about *positive thinking*. I arrive at the auditorium. In front are standing many people. Upon going to the entrance, all talk stops and everyone looks at me, making space so that I may freely enter and one opens the door for me.

Now I enter the hall where I find people gathered for the occasion. Most of them I meet for the first time. Here I have the same experience of the effect of charisma, my inner light. I talk and feel the vibration of alertness, interest and approval towards me from the audience. I have a wonderful opportunity of sharing my universal knowledge with this group. I radiate interest in my subject. This is the great gift I give first to myself in giving my understanding. I am happy within for the ability I have in explaining the essence of positive thinking.

We practitioners are masters of our life, our environment and universe. We are the charismatic figure, the living example of the meaning of charisma, the light from within.

As the sun shines out of its inner *fire* the moon and all the planets are lovely to see and seen only as they reflect the sun's inner light. If not for the sun the planets would be unseen in the void of space.

Mankind is the same as the sun. Each has an inner light sometimes called charisma. A practitioner knowingly shines out his charisma and regardless *other suns* or *planets*, the practitioner's **shine** is so outstanding it is as though all were but reflective planets to the practitioner's charisma. Dr Katarina Suter confirms this saying: *We as practitioners know that our charisma is the radiance of our nature, our divinity, and our reality which we emanate.*

Divinely Inspired Gift

*W*e ask ourselves what does charisma really mean. We look into the dictionary and find: *Divinely inspired gift, grace or talent.*

We as practitioners know that our charisma is the radiance of our nature, our divinity, and our reality which we emanate. Wherever we are we walk in the light of our own being. All we see is a reflection of our charisma. Our charisma is a torch of truth, wherever we illumine the scene with it we see love, purity, perfection, harmony and peace. We see all the qualities of our divine being reflected in our creation.

Here is an experience out of my life. A friend visited me. We sat together and had a wonderful discussion about our divine attitude. I pointed out the great learning opportunity behind each expe-

The Practitioner's Charisma

rience. I set everything in the light of positiveness. I wrapped the whole discussion in my charisma. At the end of the discussion my friend said: *I actually came to talk with you about my problems, but as I entered your home I can see only solutions!*

Our friends enter our world, our charisma, and as they do they see the reflection of our own divinity. Our charisma is the pure white light of love. We create our world in its image. We as practitioners through our charisma create each friend seeing himself as what he really is—the creator of a divinely inspired world, the creator of a world filled with positive attitudes. Just like ourselves.

Through our charisma we catalyze the divine nature of each being in our life; we inspire our creation to express its true self which is the reason we all live here on planet Earth.

Our charisma is the outer expression of what we know to be true about ourselves. Our charisma is the joy we express about our very existence.

The magic of the Pied Piper was his charisma. Oh he could play his enchanted enchanting flute and pipe the vermin into oblivion, or the town's children. The Pied Piper had charisma. He believed in himself. He had the magic of selfconfidence, charisma, and through this he created about him his world, a reflection of his thought about himself. When met with honor and integrity (his creation also) he responded in like measure. When met with disregard (his creation also) he performed another tune. In Dr Sylvia Maria Enz's illustration Herbert gave totally of himself and this utter givingness with no outer needs was responded to by all, young and old, for Herbert's charisma was in itself a *How-to-lesson* for all. Professor Enz confirms: *We can only recognize what we are* and so the hordes flocked to the piper and to Herbert and to each practitioner.

Charisma of Sincerity

Charisma is the personal magnetism, the aura, the radiance we feel about a person. I visit my spiritual sharer Herbert and experience the same situation again and again. The child of a friend is waiting with me for his father. Herbert and his dad come together and the child runs spontaneously to Herbert forgetting his dad for a moment. I experience this many times while we are sharing and discussing philosophy; he often comes and snuggles to him regardless that Herbert continues talking philosophy with me. I observe this also with other people. I often think that they are drawn into his presence as to a magnet without knowing what it is that attracts them.

We practitioners live in the awareness of our reality. We live in the purity of our inner self. We have achieved what we call the realization of selflove. We are nonjudgmental and unconditional givingness as we reach the inner state of total possessionlessness. We are like the rain. The rain falls on everything in the same way. Its purpose is to fall and in doing this it touches and blesses everything on its journey regardless of the outer appearances, everything in the same unconditional way.

Our charisma, the radiance of our inner reality shares itself in the same way to the world. We live in the aura of our original purity and integrity and express ourselves as examples of truth in all areas of our life. What we practice is keeping the awareness of who and what we are alive by seeing the purity of beingness in everybody in our world because—*we can only recognize what we are.*

Selflove is the unconditional love we share with everybody in our world as it is the aura of inner peace, love, joy and harmony we see as our reflection in everybody. And it is this purity of beingness, that reflection of our own purity that draws us into the presence of an accomplished practitioner.

Like my spiritual sharer we are wantless and needless toward any outer response and reward as we are totally selfsufficient—being and expressing what we are, God—the allness of God.

It is a common practice to work with a leader. One who conducts the meeting or program. When no leader is present someone is drafted to fill the breach because without a leader and his forceful presence group cooperation and success are seldom found. Oftentimes we seek to lay on our practitioners the responsibility of leadership. Should a practitioner ever assume a role of leadership he ceases as an effective practitioner. Truly a practitioner does not want to affect the lives of *others* and *community good*. The practitioner's first responsibility is to keep his own house, charisma, in order. Secondly the practitioner shines out as a giant beacon a light/charisma so powerful no other light or emanation is known to exist. Dr Ilse Wenk in her example points out she did the yoga exercises and meditations for herself.

Illuminated Advice: A Living Example

*W*e practitioners are those to whom friends come for spiritual guidance or for meditating or other illuminating advice. We are love and share our love with all.

A group of ladies who like myself loved yoga, wanted to practice it with me. We had our weekly meetings and enjoyed a beautiful practice of yoga. Then we found it was great to have relaxation yoga exercises. We enjoyed it very much. After we had done it for quite some time one of the ladies came to me and said: *You know, whenever you make*

The Practitioner's Charisma

these exercises with us I am so much more relaxed than doing it alone. I always look forward to when we make these exercises together. I told this lady that the reason why we made these exercises was that each one learns it individually to make these exercises alone at home. This is the reason we train.

This lady insisted, she could make these exercises only when we train it with the group. She said: *It is so beautiful when you join us to do it.*

We had a talk about charisma the other day. One friend of our group of spiritual friends talked about the charisma of our lecturer. She said that it is so easy to be in the aura of our sharer and how she feels it when she is alone and wants to keep up the beautiful vibrations she has shared with our charismatic sharer.

There is something special about practitioners. We practitioners are loved by all. We love everyone. Love is the greatest power of the universe. We are very powerful because we love. We love first ourselves and we love all our friends as we love ourselves.

The profession of being a practitioner is a beautiful activity. I love to be a practitioner.

A successful efficient practitioner is one whose charismatic self shines forth radiantly and *he does not even realize it.* The story is told of a good man who was granted one wish by God. The man said he wanted to go about doing good *without knowing about it.* God granted his wish. Then God decided this was such a noble idea, he granted that condition to all human beings. And so it is even unto today! *Noblesse oblige!* The selflessness of a practitioner, his *noblesse oblige* arising out of his totally honorable and charitable nature, the responsibility of anyone who deigns to accept the role of practitioner not realizing its great calling, happens freely and openly. The charismatic being cannot contain his charisma! Dr Robert Rettel confirms the source of charismatic activity lies in each practitioner and our expectations are indeed fulfilled.

Spiritual Maturity Our Reality

We always outpicture in our life our use of the Law of cause and effect. We create in our world that which we are, that what we think of and that of which we speak. We think very highly of ourselves and we speak very highly of everyone and we expect goodness in our life.

We recognize the beauty and abundance in *our* world as the result of *our* use of the Law of cause and effect; we recognize one power: God in us as the real supply of all good things in our world. We are a source for the divine blessings in our world.

The more we recognize this, the more we keep the channels open and the more we as the source create goodness and abundance in our world. We live constantly in the awareness of our true nature, our spiritual reality and thus we create ourselves aware we are the source, the divine presence.

We live with an attitude of spiritual maturity; we are whole in spirit, mind and body; we recognize ourselves as a spiritual being; we recognize God in us as the true supply of all the abundance of our universe; we recognize everybody as divine beings. We claim the truth about ourselves and our world: We claim purity, we claim wholeness and perfection. Even our creation of apparent contrary conditions with a new cause we claim the truth and see purity and goodness in all. We claim our innate birthright; we claim our divine reality. We are successful, prosperous in all our undertakings for we use the Law of cause and effect for our highest and best. We are the source and a catalyst of divine power. In this way we are charismatic beings; but we recognize in everyone the same divine presence, the same divine power, the same abilities, the same charismatic potentialities—us!

We recognize everyone as a charismatic being, whole, the source of the divine in them. We realize that it always comes down to application: We use the Law consciously, in the awareness of our divine reality. We claim our reality, we claim our good, we claim wholeness and perfection.

I claim the truth about myself and my world. I keep foremost in my mind that I am a spiritual being; I sing in my heart: I am God, God I am. I claim my purity, moment by moment, day by day and I see my body and my world perfect. I enjoy perfect health, a whole and perfect body.

◆

The false and the true are known to all.

Children and animals detect a sham with no words spoken, no acting made—by the pure presence of a being. Likewise the dignity of honor and reality are equally known by the naive and innocent.

Charisma is not only harmonious. Charisma is both something humanity considers negative as well as positive. A sad person lowers the vibrations of any group, while a happy person—of happy mien—exudes a charisma of delightful joyous expectations.

As a practitioner either role may be expressed.

A practitioner sent for a friend's discomfiture continues the friend's condition.

A practitioner able to program health where none seems to be; able to see spiritual dignity, where depravity lodges; able to shine forth so brightly that only his pure light is seen—such a one is a charismatic practitioner in the purest sense.

∞

Theme Fourteen

THE PRACTITIONER'S FOOD

Man is a spiritual being. All existence is consciousness.

Man may play any number of games in his human mode. He may recognize his spiritual divine heritage and be free of any possessions. These possessions include: dependency upon human relationships; control by relative physical rules including gravity, decay, aging, death, cold, heat, breathing, thirst, hunger or any sense condition; and any limitation. Or man may limit himself within the paradigm of what is human and thus be subject to all it includes.

Archetypal man is a concept free of any outside supporting influences. A selfcontained es-

The Practitioner's Food

sence dependent alone on its imagination to experience life.

Playing the game of human man evolved from its freedom to its possession of *the way it is done.* In the process man created in himself sensitivity to outside elements, a system that ingests its environment and transforms it into an assimilable state through digestion. And to further its imagination humanity—its animal self—subjects its perceptibility to a plethora of organs to utilize and need the chemical/physical responses.

Really a mental being, man says of his universe it is *food for thought.*

As practitioners our primary goal is to return in consciousness to the awareness of our archetypal reality. This is not done by denying any need. The return takes giving attention to spiritual food so completely that the day soon comes when all need or desire for the outer symbol of food has passed. All nourishment comes from the inner source.

To be an effective spiritual practitioner is not denial. It is being in harmony with all as it is. This harmony reduces the panic for the need of food, water and air. As this happens, the dire possession fades—not purposely but naturally—and the practitioner's attention is stayed on its reality allowing the domain of the real to reveal itself once again.

A practitioner's food is ideas. Pure ideas of his reality. Ideas of his archetypal self. Ideas alone.

Our practitioners herein take us step by step closer to this conception to fulfill our destiny or fate which is our divine beingness from which we only pretend to stray.

As president of three multinational corporations and abbot/abbess of the Absolute Monastery, the Rev Dr Ellen Jermini has her hands full maintaining a perfect balance of spiritual/human circumstances. So often she encounters the possession of food and things by the convent's monks and by students of the University of Healing and the University of Philosophy where she is a renowned professor and proctor. Lovingly Abbess Jermini shows the way to the archetypal reality tucked away at the heart and soul of each being. She lives her profession twenty-four hours daily.

Our Main Food in Life

*O*ur **main food in life is our spiritual food**. As we live in harmony and love with ourselves, as we concentrate on our reality in life, we use all the existing power within us. We may live for days without any food and even when trained without a drop of water. This seems tough but we know of great masters in the world that live on one kernel of rice, knowing that this is mainly a symbol of using any food.

The Practitioner's Food

We are spiritual beings, we are divine-human beings we need nothing, we want nothing as we know that we are all. We are God and we train ourselves to live what we believe.

One of our everyday practices is truly to be master of our body, master about food. What do we practitioners eat, what is our choice in food? A practitioner mainly eats everything without being possessed by any food at any time yet making a choice as e.g. vegetables and fruits rather than meat. We practitioners determine what we want out of life as we know that we are the creators of our world and any circumstance in life.

We live in a physical body and give this physical body food to exist. We participate in the game of meals; such as breakfast, lunch and dinner and sit down with our fellowmen sharing a cheerful time of togetherness. Our thoughts determine any necessity of food, our thoughts decide for us what is healthy and good.

So I recall a visit with a friend of mine living several days in my house, refusing food kept some days in the refrigerator. She tells me that this is old and bad food which destroys the body, she says that makes her sick. I explain to her that this is an old idea which truly refers to her childhood or her education but with changing her attitude about the food she can eat everything. I also share my daily prayer with her, the blessing I give to any food before putting it into my mouth. I pray: **This food** (and I name the food in detail) **is healthy for my body and filled with love**. I explain to her that with my treatment I definitely put a positive cause into motion and it works. I say, it is done unto our belief.

At that very moment this lady is utterly amazed about my way of thinking and she finally understands and participates in the game. She eats the food I offer her. Later she gives her recognition to me, she says that she has learned a wise lesson and she now understands that all is thought, all is attitude in life.

Responsibility is the key Dr Stefan Strässle insists be used to control the substance seemingly required by the body to function. Since we feel we must eat to remain alive Professor Strässle directs our thinking to the concept of all we eat being whole and beneficial to the functioning of our organism. A technique each practitioner utilizes is the prayer treatment: *THIS FOOD IS HEALTHY FOR MY BODY AND FILLED WITH LOVE!*

Bless What We Eat

*A*s practitioners we always take charge of our world and experiences. To be totally in control of our life also means that we take responsibility for the food we eat.

We practitioners know that any responsibility is a matter of our consciousness. We conceive of the perfect attitude regarding the food we eat and in this way take full charge. We empower the

The Practitioner's Food

perfect attitude by speaking a powerful prayer before eating food of any kind. We may say: **This food is healthy for my body and filled with love.**

A positive affirmation sets the Law of cause and effect into motion to our positive benefit. All the food we bless and eat thereafter is especially surrounded with love and absolutely good and perfect for our body in every aspect. The blessed food we eat is in perfect harmony with our digestion, assimilation, circulation and elimination.

To bless anything we eat, in whatever circumstances we find ourselves, is truly the key to the purity and perfection in our body.

It reminds me of a trip I plan through Mexico. I talk to friends about it and they tell me many beautiful things about the country and the Mexican people. It sounds all so inviting! However, someone tells me to be very careful with the food I eat because of its uncleanliness and its being filled with bacteria causing severe stomach problems. I am told to only eat chosen food and to only drink water or sodas out of bottles because of the malaria I could catch. I get the advice to take tablets to protect myself. Oh, I hear all sorts of limiting comments. However, within myself I know the truth and I apply the skills of a perfect practitioner. Being in Mexico I eat and drink whatever I have a desire for, without thinking that the food or the drinks are unclean or filled with bacteria. *Everytime* before I eat or drink I bless the meal and experience perfect results—a pure and perfect body.

PRACTITIONERS MANUAL

This is how we practitioners act relative to the food we eat and the water we drink. Always we return to our own thought, to our own inward attitude. **There** *we make things happen in our lives*, **only there**. It is always done unto us according to our belief. And it works perfectly.

A humanist, Dr Ingeborg Puchert looks about her creation and sees all things there to sublimate the divine relative and the relative divine. Knowing full well all is thought, the body and the experience, Professor Puchert points out that so long as we live on the relative level of consciousness we may as well have fun and enter into the game of eating earthly substances for the joy of it—certainly not the necessity of it!

Eat For the Fun of It

The practitioner lives in spirit.

The form of the fleshly body is the expression of what is in the consciousness of the practitioner. The physical body is the true outpicturing of that form which is brought into being through thought. All is thought and thought expresses as appearances in the relative world.

The physical food of the practitioner, which is also spiritual, consists of material food, the mani-

249

The Practitioner's Food

festation of universal substance. The material food the practitioner takes is utilized on a limited reference.

The practitioner is the expression of universal energy and gives life to himself from within. Humanity claims material food is a kind of vehicle through which the fleshly body is maintained through the spirit within.

The practitioner lives consciously in the spiritual realm where all things just are. It is fun for the practitioner to play this relative game of eating and drinking material substances called food.

I live in the awareness that wherever I am I am supplied with the things for my physical support.

I think of a special dish and a friend invites me to a famous restaurant where it is served, that special Chinese dish of fried mixed fish. I accept the visit of a ladyfriend and I receive a delicious homemade cheesecake. What else can I want or wish? In these gifts I recognize the reward of spiritual knowingness of the abundance of food in my world.

On my property I enjoy the source of pure water, this water I channel into a pipe to a faucet and drink of it all the time. In this unlimited source I see the universal, spiritual source of life.

Freely in nature I gather green leaves which are eatable. I know the mulberry, almond, elderberry, buckwheat and more.

This is the universal principle of givingness, I give freely of my knowledge and substance and experience an unlimited return of goods.

All life is the continuous exchange of blessings in giving and receiving in an unlimited measure.

All this I also define as the practitioner's food.

The dynamic words we use to describe the sustenance enjoyed by our bodies and the purpose of this sustenance we consciously conceive are our reality. Dr Katarina Suter specifically cites: *The food is without any quality in itself, we give it the quality through speaking our positive word.* The game we allow food to play in our bodies or the lack of control we give to food as a game to play in our bodies is a decision we alone approve.

Absolute Creators of Our World

*I*t is important to know that we as a practitioner are the absolute creator of our world. Whatever we create is good and very good. This is true for the practitioner's food.

We bless the food *before* we eat it. Wherever we are and whatever we eat, we call our food *healthy for our body and filled with love*. **The food is without any quality in itself, we give it the quality through speaking our positive word**. We put the cause into motion and experience the effect.

The Practitioner's Food

I travel in Bali, a wonderful island of the Republic of Indonesia. Most of the food I eat is new to me. I stay at a little inn with a small kitchen. Adjacent or almost in the kitchen are a few pigs which are fed with the discarded food. Right behind the kitchen in the back yard are a few simple cottages one of which is my home. Everytime I go from the road to my cottage I walk through the kitchen, seeing all the flies and bugs doing their work.

In the morning the servant knocks at my cottage door and sets my breakfast in front of it—a banana and a pot with hot tea and brown sugar! I pick up the tray and tell a few bugs to go and look for their food somewhere else. I sit on the stairs and bless my food. Wherever I eat and drink, on the highway or in a restaurant, I create the food healthy for my body and filled with love. Through the whole trip I feel perfectly healthy and I am without the need for any tablet. My tablet is my positive thought.

Through this example we may realize the freedom we create for ourselves through the conscious use of the Law of cause and effect. We are perfectly satisfied and fulfilled with whatever food we create—strange or known to us, a little or a lot. We know that the thought about our creation is what fulfills us. We know that our body is the temple of the living God and all we nourish it with is healthy and filled with love. We have a perfect diet—our positive thought about our creation.

Could a practitioner create substance negative to his highest good? No. Could a practitioner create substance positive to his highest good? No. A practitioner can only create an *isness*, or an *experience* in his life. For each happening is viewed by the practitioner for what he chooses to make of it through his attitude. Hence Dr Sylvia Maria Enz chose to create conditions through her pseudo ignorance and through her pseudo awareness she desires to experience. The edge is very fine wherein the choice takes place.

I Remember . . . Yuck!

*T*he one thing to remember before talking about the value of food in our life is to always be aware that **we as practitioners of truth are the only creators of our world**. The Law of cause and effect works in all areas of our beingness.

I *remember* a situation when I was living with friends in an apartment in Switzerland. I was hungry when I came home from work. In the darkness of the night I opened the fridge to look for something to eat. In the back I found a bowl with something that looked like a leftover dessert. I ate it with good appetite although I found it had a rather strange taste. Two days later I mentioned to my girlfriend that I had eaten the rest of the dessert—and saw her incredulous face as she told me that it was old and full of mold—ready to be thrown away. The moment she said this I felt my stomach turning upside down and with my whole body I felt a strong feeling of disgust. Later I thought about this situation and that at the moment I ate the spoiled food I felt perfect and also later I was without a strange reaction in my body.

This illustration tells us so very clearly that everything we experience we create by our thought. Everything we eat is exactly as good or as bad, as tasty or as stale, as we believe it to be. We as practitioners know that everything is good in the spiritual reality, everything is intrinsically perfect, whole and pure. To arrive at this point however needs programing our consciousness to this reality awareness.

We as practitioners at the Absolute Monastery practice this awareness by blessing everything we eat *aloud*. Every item on the plate we bless by saying: The bread and the butter and the milk and the jam and the peanut butter is healthy for my body and filled with love. We say this as a confirmation that everything we as practitioners of spiritual truth eat, is beneficial and harmonious with our body; we affirm that everything is as healthy as we create it—by our thought, by our attitude about it.

To the pure all is pure. Whatever we experience with the purity and love of our true self is good for our wellbeing, on the physical, mental and spiritual level. We experience the reality of the oneness we are in, as and through everything.

Dr Ilse Wenk describes a practitioner's food! The source of our nourishment is our spirit, is our consciousness. This source is abundant. It is never ending. This source is infinite.

A Practitioner's Food

*T*he *practitioner's food is love, joy, understanding and all the other virtues which are offered by our choice to enjoy life. We nourish ourselves by the constant meditation. We are always in a meditative state.*

Meditation means to think about. That means that we always think conscious and onepointed thoughts which are our most precious food. We nourish ourselves from what we are, from what we have. We are selfsustained. We think good thoughts, speak good words and do good deeds.

The source of our nourishment is our spirit, is our consciousness. This source is abundant. It is never ending. This source is infinite.

We are the first thought. We are the first cause. Out of this first cause, this first thought, we live our life.

The eternal light is our thought of love. It is through illumination that our spirit nourishes itself.

Our food is givingness. It is as when the gardener takes his big scissors to cut the leaves of the tree or the plant to let it grow

The Practitioner's Food

better. Whenever we give, whenever we share our love with our friends, our light grows, our love increases, our life is more beautiful than ever before. Our food is sharing with all our friends. We share our love and understanding, we share our joy, we share our happiness.

The basis of our food supply is our never ending practice and training of diligence, determination, dedication, discipline, onepointedness and humility. With this practice we stay alert and vivid.

We practitioners are always fulfilled. We are the masters of our body, mind and soul. We practice acceptance. And that is beautiful and brings us so much joy. We live in the light of the divine, of the infinite and pour out our love in this beautiful light. We are the light, the way and the truth.

Dr Robert Rettel recognizes two human choices for food; and the only realm the practitioner works within, **the spiritual realm**. He describes both levels of awareness with a keen alertness of the professor he is expounding on the apparent duality of life all the while fully conscious of the only oneness.

We Live in a Community of Thought

We take care of our body by eating proper food, by drinking pure liquids and relaxing. We eat natural foods, we drink pure water, we rest our body by relaxing all our muscles. We recognize the importance of taking care of our body in a physical way.

More important is to take care of the thoughts about our body and more generally, all our thoughts. For we create our world *in the first place* by the thoughts that we think, we create our body by the thoughts we have about it. We realize that it is important to eat proper, fresh food; but *more important is every thought that we think and every word that we speak.* For by every thought and every word we put the Law of cause and effect in motion for us and our entire universe.

We realize the importance of our attitude; we keep a pure attitude of mind. We keep a joyous mind all day long; we are constantly in a happy, balanced state.

We take control of all our thoughts; we think thoughts of joy, abundance, peace and harmony.

We think pure thoughts for our body: We see it strong, we see it whole and perfect. We visualize every function, organ and action in a perfect state.

Before we eat, we bless our meals and fill them with divine love. We think thoughts of love, of peace and harmony. We see our love in all people, all the beings in our world. We are in a peaceful state as we eat. We are in harmony with ourselves and our universe, we are at peace. We eat properly; we keep our thoughts pure.

We eat proper food in a physical, mental and spiritual way. In the physical world we eat pure, fresh and healthy food. In our mental world we take care of our thoughts. We always think posi-

The Practitioner's Food

tively and constructively. In a spiritual way we are aware of our divine nature.

I take loving care of my body with proper food, pure liquids and total relaxation. I think pure thoughts about my body. By every pure thought I feed the body, I create a healthy, whole and perfect body. All day long I think well of my body; I bless every part of it and see it as the temple of the living God.

◆

Our professional practitioners from throughout the world reveal an awareness that the usual concept of food means physical substance—but they would draw the friend into the reality domain wherein all exists.

Formulae abound for the ultimate meal.

All formulae which suggest limitation and finiteness can be easily recognized as leading away from the spiritual goals practitioners establish for themselves.

All formulae which start with the infinite and expand from there take consciousness *home* to its reality domain wherein it recognizes its fullness and never more hungers.

For our benefit the practitioners toyed with both extremes. The obvious FOOD of a PRACTITIONER is spiritual substance. Anything else on any physical, human, material level only leads to annihilation.

Practitioners spend their entire lives feasting at the font of life, purity, joy, truth, using the Law for every choice! ∞

PROCESS IMMEDIATELY

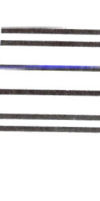

BUSINESS REPLY MAIL

FIRST-CLASS MAIL PERMIT NO. 15590 LOS ANGELES CA

POSTAGE WILL BE PAID BY ADDRESSEE

**SCIENCE OF MIND
PO BOX 18087
ANAHEIM CA 92817-9942**

NO POSTAGE
NECESSARY
IF MAILED
IN THE
UNITED STATES

Science of Mind®

A philosophy, a faith, a way of life

Subscribe and save!

☐ 1 year (12 issues) for just $19.95

That's more than **43%** off the cover price!

Name _____

Address _____

City _____

State _____ Zip _____

☐ Please bill me.

For faster service or credit card orders, call 1-800-247-6463.

Please allow 6-8 weeks for first issue.

Theme Fifteen

THE PRACTITIONER'S GOAL

*T*he goal of every created being in the universe is to fulfill its awareness of who and what it is!

All is God. All is the absolute. In through and as all is all. Wherever the absolute is all that the absolute is is present in its allness. So regardless a stone, an ear of corn, a beetle, a cow, a barn, a house or a man: each is all of God, all of the all, expressing itself in the isness as that which it expresses at the moment. Important to remember: isness is at the point it is aware of its isness. What we call evolution is merely isness in a stage of awareness of itself. Should *isness* ever be aware of itself as *allness* it would cease to be the isness it sees itself as.

The Practitioner's Goal

As the ultimate goal of a practitioner is fulfilled it knows who and what it is: allness. Being the absolute allness it no longer knows of itself as a human, animal, mineral, vegetable—nothing or something—it then is all!

This heavenly state of bliss is full. All pseudo emptiness is lost and we live in our divine self.

At each point of light, our illumination was to be the best for ourselves. In our ultimate goal we are all, there is no best!

A modest ultimate master Dr Ellen Jermini is magnificently able to live *in* the world knowing full well her absolute nature therein refraining from being *of* the Earth and its game. She lives in her diapason self expressing her full range of her absolute self as a divine-human being. As she reveals by her life that creating her own world in her perfect pure image is a pleasure devoutly to behold.

I Remember Who and What I AM!

We all are practitioners and following our heart's desire we know that our only purpose in life is to remember who and what we are and to be it. This purpose automatically fulfills our final goal in life as we live in the awareness of our reality, as we live our divine self.

In order to achieve a goal—any goal in life, we practice discipline, dedication, determination and diligence in all what we do for the fun of doing it, for the fun of our beingness. We onepointedly direct our thoughts on that which we have in mind to achieve—on our great goal—and visualize it done; we live in the awareness that it is accomplished. So we think our thoughts, we speak our words and deal with our fellowmen in a gentle loving way the same way as we like to be treated, *creating our world in our pure perfect image.*

Speaking of goal, I remember myself as a fanatic tennis player, fanatic in so far as I put all my attention on my goal as a winner of the game I participate in. I recall myself getting up in the morning while immediately mentally entering the tennis court. Here I stand in front of my partner of the day knowing his tactic in the game, but myself knowing perfectly the rules by which I have to play. I visualize myself giving the best, giving one hundred percent of myself to the required game knowing and recognizing myself as the winner of the match. I play well but without being in competition with my fellowman. I play for the fun of participating in the game and to achieve **my goal being the best of myself.**

We practitioners play by the rules of life, the rules are to be disciplined, dedicated, determined and diligent *players* participating in the game of life onepointedly directed on the truth of beingness. We are the masters and the creators of our world and through our thoughts we live nonjudgmentally, unconditionally in humility as our divine self.

The Practitioner's Goal

We know our final goal in life, we know our rules to play by, we know that we are God, the absolute, one as all, we know that we are one as the goal, **we know that we are that we are!**

The concept goal, perilous as it is to understand, when understood, can be smoothly fulfilled by every onepointed being. Dr Stefan Strässle clearly delineates the skills necessary to fully utilize the metaphysical principle of the universe, the tool of its service, the Law of cause and effect. Dr Strässle assures us *we are all practitioners.*

Be Onepointed!

A goal is the most important thing to which any person could aspire. It is the essence of life. A goal is giving a meaning and purpose to life. A goal sets all the creative energy within us into motion to inspire and to bring forth genius and its unlimited reservoir of ideas to fulfill our imagination.

There exist innumerable goals to which we might aspire. All of us have free choice to claim any goal we desire. We have the capacity to achieve anything and always be successful for we all use the Law of cause and effect—used by the universal principle by which all is created—to reach the goal we set into motion for ourselves.

Since every being on planet Earth and in the entire universe uses the Law to create his world, to accomplish his goal, *we are all practitioners*. We are all practitioners of the Law of cause and effect. *This is the primary purpose we are here: to use the tool (the Law) to accomplish our dreams.*

To accomplish any goal is an easy task. As practitioners we remain true to our goal, which means that the goal/dream is ALWAYS on our heart and we put its fulfillment above anything else so our dream manifests. This is the Law. Anything we onepointedly put our attention on manifests in our world. Wherever our disciplined, motivated thought *is* **is** our experience. The Law of cause and effect works unfailingly.

I remember myself being a little boy of five years old. My dream, my goal was to become a successful soccer player. I gave my full attention to playing soccer and playing it successfully. As it is with a dream or a goal that really comes as an inspiration from the heart, the fulfillment is easily manifested because practicing is fun and learning discipline which is necessary to achieve the goal is a pleasure. So it was with my career as a soccer player. Everything was easy because I lived my dream/goal. I played and practiced for fun. Even the demanding practicing hours in the soccer club over the years were fun for I always tasted the fulfillment of the dream with every game I played. And really, year by year I polished my skills successfully in every area of the game. I played in soccer leagues where according to my age I was too young to play; however, because of the perfect skills I performed I convinced the coaches. I achieved my dream for I stayed true to my goal. I

The Practitioner's Goal

put the goal to be a skilled soccer player above anything else and thereby put the Law perfectly into motion to bring forth the effect.

We all have examples of how powerfully and precisely the Law works. The accomplishment of any goal lies in the heart of ourselves alone. We truly achieve our innermost dreams, regardless the circumstances. Our lives outpicture exactly what we think.

Everyone describes the journey to experience who and what they are: few have it clearly understood hence few arrive at the demonstration of their heart's goal. Dr Ingeborg Puchert declares with the totality of her being: *We are spiritual practitioners.* Ultimately, Professor Puchert insists, we recognize the divine whispering to us and it is our own voice. A confirmation on the journey that the goal, like the voice, resides within each of us alone and only there will we find our reality.

THE Voice Is My Voice

*W*e *are spiritual practitioners.* We know who we are, we affirm we are all that we imagine about ourselves and are it. We are one as the God presence within us.

While living on planet Earth we know where our real home is. We consciously live from within and mentally visualize our real existence in the boundless universe. This is our inner strength through which we achieve every goal we set up for ourselves in our world.

We play the role of a human being wellknowing our divine reality. We feel the urge from within and put a definite cause in motion for the achievement of our goal which is being universal oneness. This is the inner call and we thoroughly listen to that gentle whispering voice, through our own voice. We realize that this is the highest, the ultimate goal of all goals ever envisaged.

We accept this challenge and spiritually prepare ourselves for the glorious reunion with our reality. Although this trip to our final existence in the universe is a lonely one yet the reward is priceless and unique.

I talk about my own search for the light, the truth and real fulfillment of my desires, my goal. I think of my attempts to understand the interpretations of the Bible, of the many books about religious and spiritual knowledge without seeing any purpose in them for me. I take yoga lessons and feel balanced.

Without grand expectations I make the trip by train to another town where for the first time I am asked to attend a special philosophical seminar. Although the subject is totally new for me, I find it interesting. I begin with the study of the correspondence course of this philosophy and experience a miracle. For the first time in my life I hear the sound of silver bells ringing about me. I am in

The Practitioner's Goal

heaven. I commit myself to this uplifting philosophy. I take another trip and now I am at the meditation center of the Absolute Monastery in Campo, California. Now I am a practitioner and live in the fulfillment of my first goal. The next goal is the ultimate journey into the infinite reality of my beingness, which varies from the previous trips in Europe by train, car and airplane to the USA.

I leave behind the sense of possession and I am there. In doing this I have a clear view of what I am doing and how to master the tests I create along the way to the final destination. I am fearless to see the light that I am. I illumine the way with my inner bright light. I make one step and take hold where I am and prepare myself for the next step.

I live in timelessness. I start this trip and see myself being there and in this knowingness I am my goal. Indeed, we practitioners see in this ultimate experience the final goal for ourselves.

Many practitioners confuse their dreams and desires with their ultimate goal in life: to know who and what they are. Dr Katarina Suter tells how fulfilling our dreams prepare us in using the virtues of discipline, humility, onepointedness, dedication, diligence and determination in the application of the Law of cause and effect in the area of our ultimate goal. Thus a conscious master fulfills his goal.

To Be or Not to Be a Farmer

*W*e as practitioners know that having a goal in life is very important. We also know that each being on planet Earth has ultimately the same goal. *The goal is being the absolute master of our life and expressing it.* This is the reason why we as a practitioner, and everyone is a practitioner, choose this experience on planet Earth.

During our training of being an absolute master we choose temporary dreams, dreams which stand as a symbol for the ultimate goal. Through these dreams we learn all the qualities required to enter the state of an absolutely aware master. We call these qualities discipline, humility, onepointedness, dedication, diligence and determination.

I think of a dream I had in my childhood. I love farming—I love everything which has to do with animals and nature. I spent all my holidays on the farm of a family friend. After school until supper was ready I spent my time at the neighbor's farm. At home I cut the little grass behind the house with a sickle and dried it. I kept the hay in a big wooden crate imagining that a rider with a hungry horse would pass by and enjoy my harvest. I spent my whole time with thoughts about farming. As I left school I chose farming as my profession.

Through my absolute onepointedness, discipline, dedication and constant visualization as a child I achieved the dream of being a great farmer.

The choice of the goal is important. Our use of the Law of cause and effect is a vital tool for the

The Practitioner's Goal

achievement of spiritual qualities. Our one hundred percent dedication to the chosen goal brings miracles in all areas of our life. We are like this little girl who loves farming; we spend every instant of our life with thinking, visualizing and living the goal we choose, for what we think is what we are and what we experience.

We fulfill every chosen dream totally and to our highest and best. This way we create the greatest learning experience in discipline, humility, onepointedness, dedication, determination and diligence, true qualities of a conscious master, our ultimate goal!

The temptation of humanity is to equate relative experiences with the same definition we use for our reality nature. In doing this we and future generations stand confused and ineffectual. Dr Sylvia Maria Enz points out how our human destinations can be likened to our ultimate goal of being our real self, but it is not the real thing. However, the concepts of being tempted and sidetracked on our journey to awareness are similar and offer themselves as indicators of our turning in fruitless ways to ineffective meanderings. Ours is a specific course to a specific goal incomparable!

The Ultimate Journey

*T*o practice means to exercise a skill we choose to live. To practice also means that we live what we believe is true about ourselves. We practitioners know that our purpose for being on this dimension of experience is to become aware of our real self—and as the definition of this awareness—living it, being it.

As practitioners of truth we have determined the path on the journey to our inner awareness ourselves. This can be easily demonstrated with an illustration. We plan a trip, let's say to the redwoods. Once we have determined this destination we visualize ourselves there. Regardless of the apparent distance we have to cover, in our thought, in our awareness we have arrived there. We know the destination and whatever we do on the trip—we know where we are going. We start the journey by car and on the way we are compelled to stop and look at the many beautiful sights. Depending on our eagerness to arrive at the redwoods we let ourselves be tempted to stop here and there to enjoy the beauty of a scenery, the company of lovely people. Or both! All the while we are aware of our destination. All these little sidetracks are an enrichment and joy as long as we have the redwoods and the purpose of the redwoods clearly in mind. Often we let ourselves be tempted to stay longer at a place and then we push ourselves to continue the journey by visualizing the destination once again. We see ourselves hiking through the woods; we marvel at the lushness of the trees and bushes. We hear the wind

The Practitioner's Goal

moving the treetops, a symphony of harmony and serenity.

This simple illustration is an exact parallel to the spiritual path. We are born into this adventure on planet Earth with the clearly determined *goal of being aware of who and what we are. Wherever our journey to this awareness leads us we always know where we are going. Within ourselves we always know who we are.* So, regardless of how many sidetracks into the human sensative world we choose to experience, the primary task of us practitioners is to know that **we are always there.** We practice the awareness of **being there** and we make our trip a fun experience because we know that all what we experience is a selfcreated illusion, as we always are that what we are.

Oh yes, the journey to the goal is fun and should we tempt ourselves to stay too long on a sidetrack we go within and find there the clear picture of the beauty of our goal, the clear awareness of our reality. As skilled practitioners we live totally and constantly in this awareness regardless of appearances we create in our physical world.

The happiest being in the universe is a practitioner. A practitioner has no responsibility for anything. A practitioner first sees himself aware of who and what he is and in so doing the practitioner sees all his creation fulfilled, according to Dr Ilse Wenk. Professor Wenk further states we are here to *enjoy our life*!

Practitioners Share How To Reveal Ourselves

*O*ur goal as practitioners is to know who and what we are. To always be our true and pure selves, to live our divine beingness with all our heart and all our soul. Along the way to love our neighbor as ourselves. For we are the greatest servant of all.

Our goal is to work daily on the accomplishment of our inner bliss, to enjoy every moment of our life: *we are here on this planet Earth to remember who and what we are and to enjoy our life.*

My dream as a child was already to be a perfect pianist. I dreamt it. I visualized it. I saw me as a great artist. I practiced the piano with onepointedness, determination, diligence, discipline and dedication. I remembered practicing Beethoven's *Für Elise* until I played it excellently and was a great success. I shared my love with all. Love sharing is my greatest bliss.

Practitioners accomplish any task with onepointedness, determination, diligence, discipline and dedication.

We share all our love with all our friends.

We always are totally concerned only with our own state of awareness and recognize that the world we live in is now whole and perfect. In this integrity we treat.

The Practitioner's Goal

Our principle function is to practice spiritual revelation, spiritual purity and spiritual mind treatment.

One of our programs is to show the friends who come to us for treatment how to reveal themselves. We all live according to the one Law. It is the Law of cause and effect. Each one is living coeternally with this universal Law. We all are the first cause and the only cause. Every thought we think is a cause and the effect is always the result of the thought. We say we are happy beautiful beings. We are full of love for ourselves and our fellowmen. We are happy and joyful at all times. And while we say it and think it, we are it. We are the positive thinkers.

My program in working with my creation is that all my friends who come to me use the Law of cause and effect to reveal themselves.

Creation is the theme of Dr Robert Rettel as he describes the goal of creation to remember who and what it is! We can only be effective in working with our own creation, Professor Rettel insists, but in this, because we are so apparently aware of the human role, *we create a fantastic world so marvelous, perfect and pure that it is heaven on this planet Earth.* Indeed we are royalty and wielding our scepter of authority we create an awareness of who and what we are masterfully.

The King and His Scepter

*W*e as practitioner are concerned with our own state of awareness. We recognize our whole world, our creation, as pure. In this pure state of integrity we *treat* for ourselves and our world: we put causes in motion. In this high state we always see the truth and thus we create beauty, harmony, purity and love for our entire universe.

As practitioner we consciously create our world. We keep out thoughts on our goal, our awareness of *who and what we are*, of **who and what our (creation) fellow people are.** We see ourselves constantly as divine beings; we see in everyone the highest expression: God. We see beyond apparent limitations and see freedom. We see beauty, peace, joy and purity for all in our entire universe. We create a fantastic world so marvelous, perfect and pure that it is heaven on this planet Earth. We live in the here and now, in total knowingness of our divine birthright. We take the royal scepter and rule over our entire universe by our positive thoughts. We are the king and we rule with wisdom, with love, with *understanding of who and what we are*. We control our world by our pure thoughts; we direct our proper ruling by our perfect thoughts and our perfect words.

As practitioner we give expression to our pure nature; we express totally and beautifully our Godself.

As a practitioner I turn to the limitlessness of my true nature; I control my world from the mental

The Practitioner's Goal

plane. I put supportive causes in motion: I see beauty, harmony and purity. I create wholeness and perfection in every situation.

I create heaven on Earth, here and now, for me and my entire world. I create in my consciousness a beautiful, whole and perfect world, a pristine pure world. I look at my world and I see purity and perfection.

◆

The *Practitioner's Goal* to know who and what he is and to be that who and which he is sounds so remote and unattainable; but only unreachable to those whose sense of adventure is lacking; only to those who have lost all motivation to dream and mentally soar to the neverneverland of imagination and creatively drawn illusions of the fantasy of reality.

Only as each of us enter the arena of dreams, imagination and illusion will we reveal the joyful excitement of who and what we really are.

Philosopher kings throughout written history repeat the imaginative concept of *lift up your eyes unto the hills* for *the stones have voices and will be heard* and all existence has a story to tell.

Our staid scientists could not but yet did somehow gather their stoic community about them to say out of the nothing the first atom came forth from some intelligence to expand into all the substance of the universe, and at some point, involute, returning to lesser and lesser substance (as in a black hole) until once again it is but one atom and then nothing yet again! Wow what an imagination inspired this, however it corresponds with all known scientific principles known to date.

Who are we! What are we! We are the allness. So let's take it from there to fulfill our reality domain goal. ∞

CONCLUSION

*W*e can only open the door leading to spiritual grandeur. The desire to pursue this ultimate noble calling must upwell from the very depths of the individual consciousness to provide the participant with an appreciation of what it means to have an illuminated awareness and be it.

All existence is because the Law of cause and effect is initiated.

There are stages of awareness of efficient practitioners.

- The *fulfilled stage* could be likened to a composer/performer. The music that soars through his soul is captured in notes and clefs, and he has the technical genius with an instrument to reveal it.

- The *illumined stage* could be likened to a performer who cannot compose, or a composer who cannot play. The awareness is there in part but it is not complete.

- The *aware stage* is likened to a being who loves music but cannot compose or play.

- The *asleep stage* is where one is deaf to the music, or who hearing it calls it noise or undifferentiated sound.

Conclusion

The Practitioner

*T*he practitioner is one who appreciates each stage in the progress of awareness. The practitioner does not belittle where one is in consciousness. The practitioner is thrilled at each stage and delighted at any attempt to understand the deeper awareness and further progress of any being on the way.

From the asleep stage wherein dwell the majority of life, the practitioner watches over the resters knowing full well they will arise. Each like a plant seed has within the genius which one day will burst forth. The caring practitioner at all times keeps his vision on the unseen reality within each. As it comes forth, to the practitioner, it is no surprise.

Each aware, illumined, or fulfilled practitioner works with those who come just before his stage of consciousness. His proximity to his brother gives him a sensitivity to the stage from which he so recently arose.

It is no grand ego achievement to be at a particular stage. For in the timelessness we dwell in any one stage for but the blink of an eye and we are the composer and the performer—for ourselves.

None can judge for we express for ourselves alone.

Consider a glowing symphony concert. As we sit in the concert hall all is designed to transport each guest to spheres of unimagined beauty. A man holds his wife's hand. Each are dressed in their finery for an evening out. A glaze comes over their eyes. Each one separately is in their body alone. As the music of the symphony paints its melodious pictures, the wife sees her visions, the husband sees his. They profess they are one yet in this moment of the majestical magic of music each flies a separate journey. No words can express it and no images could paint the wonder experienced.

In like manner the practitioner as a professional transporter moves his counselees or friends into their own inner realm. Neither the practitioner nor his friend know what the other is doing but by his charisma the practitioner helps to break down the barriers of awareness.

The practitioner does not make something happen.

The professional sharer provides the mental atmosphere in which illumination can take place.

Beauty and harmony have long been recognized as that to which the sleeping should awaken to so that their awareness transition may be complete and immediate.

To awaken to lovely music in an idealic setting is conducive to experiencing illumination.

Many parents intuitively know this and seek this for their children with lovely surroundings in their room and the smell of wholesome tasty food and happy voices to allure the young to sharing. What sage practitioners are these parents. Can anyone say what goes on within these children— the cause has its effect in selfsufficient children harmonious with their world and expressing illumined awareness.

This Volume

*I*n this volume we have sought to enthuse and excite the imagination through the use of many voices from these efficient successful professional practitioners telling tales from their experience.

We will surely read many more books on this subject and we will be amazed by the growing facts science reveals each day. Ultimately we will come to the conclusion—in fact—all is thought.

Science laid before us the *Big Bang* theory of creation of an intelligence out of nothing bringing forth the first atom which became the material universe and returned to its nothingness; or the walking on *fire* and not being burned. This is contrary to the laws of physics because these are not laws, they are but relative rules which change as other relative rules are exercised. Each thought being a cause leading to an effect in the grand Law, the Law of cause and effect or thought!

A professional practitioner knows that all is possible, all is probable, all is. For anything that is capable of being thought is capable of being—for it already is or it could not have been thought.

Indeed we are working with something beyond our words to describe or explain. All we know is that the professional practitioner works in a realm even he cannot describe. Ask the Buddha to explain Nirvana and he will only be able to say it is extreme bliss. Ask Jesus the Christ to reveal Heaven and he will be at a loss for words. Ask Socrates to define infinite awareness and he will ask you a question in return revealing your understanding of the subject. Ask Shakespeare how he could write so widely and decisively yet with such awareness and compassion and he will say an inner scribe wrote he but moved the pen.

Who and what is this inner scribe we would all like to know. Who? It is our oneness as God the omniscient, the absolute, the all.

Books of philosophy toy with these topics.

We as would-be professional practitioners work solely with our heart and mind. All input from outside ourself is misleading. All output from within ourself is divine and revealing.

Trust this inner giant, the genius residing in each of us, and as we do our talent as illumined practitioners will grow and grow to such a point that we give it no further thought and just are!

We will no longer build bridges for others to cross over the chasm of life, we will be . . . .

(You fill in the missing word here and you will know upon which stage which you stand and upon which you perform.) ∞